The rapid growth of academic literature in the field of economics has posed serious problems for both students and teachers of the subject. The latter find it difficult to keep pace with more than a few areas of their subject, so that an inevitable trend towards specialism emerges. The student quickly loses perspective as the maze of theories and models grows and the discipline accommodates an increasing amount of quantitative techniques.

'Macmillan Studies in Economics' is a new series which sets out to provide the student with short, reasonably critical surveys of the developments within the various specialist areas of theoretical and applied economics. At the same time, the studies aim to form an integrated series so that, seen as a whole, they supply a balanced overview of the subject of economics. The emphasis in each study is upon recent work, but each topic will generally be placed in a historical context so that the reader may see the logical development of thought through time. Selected bibliographies are provided to guide readers to more extensive works. Each study aims at a brief treatment of the salient problems in order to avoid clouding the issues in detailed argument. Nonetheless, the texts are largely self-contained, and presume only that the student has some knowledge of elementary micro-economics and macro-economics.

Mathematical exposition has been adopted only where necessary. Some recent developments in economics are not readily comprehensible without some mathematics and statistics, and quantitative approaches also serve to shorten what would otherwise be lengthy and involved arguments. Where authors have found it necessary to introduce mathematical techniques, these techniques have been kept to a minimum. The emphasis is upon the economics, and not upon the quantitative methods. Later studies in the series will provide analyses of the links between quantitative methods, in particular econometrics, and economic analysis.

MACMILLAN STUDIES IN ECONOMICS

General Editors: D. C. ROWAN and G. R. FISHER

Executive Editor: D. W. PEARCE

Published

John Burton: WAGE INFLATION
Miles Fleming: MONETARY THEORY
C. J. Hawkins and D. W. Pearce: CAPITAL INVESTMENT APPRAISAL
David F. Heathfield: PRODUCTION FUNCTIONS
D. W. Pearce: COST-BENEFIT ANALYSIS
David Robertson: INTERNATIONAL TRADE POLICY
R. Shone: THE PURE THEORY OF INTERNATIONAL TRADE
Frank J. B. Stilwell: REGIONAL ECONOMIC POLICY
Grahame Walshe: INTERNATIONAL MONETARY REFORM

Forthcoming

E. R. Chang: PRINCIPLES OF ECONOMIC ACCOUNTING
G. Denton: ECONOMICS OF INDICATIVE PLANNING
N. Gibson: MONETARY POLICY
C. J. Hawkins: THEORY OF THE FIRM
D. Jackson: ACCOUNTING FOR POVERTY
P. N. Junankar: INVESTMENT FUNCTIONS
J. E. King: LABOUR ECONOMICS
J. Kregel: THEORY OF ECONOMIC GROWTH
D. Mayston: THE POSSIBILITY OF SOCIAL CHOICE
G. McKenzie: MONETARY THEORY OF INTERNATIONAL TRADE
S. K. Nath: WELFARE ECONOMICS
A. Peaker: BRITISH ECONOMIC GROWTH SINCE 1945
F. Pennance: HOUSING ECONOMICS
Maurice Peston: PUBLIC GOODS AND THE PUBLIC SECTOR
C. Rowley: ANTI-TRUST ECONOMICS
C. Sharp: TRANSPORT ECONOMICS
G. K. Shaw: FISCAL POLICY
P. Simmons: DEMAND THEORY
M. Stabler: AGRICULTURAL ECONOMICS
M. Townsend: MONETARISM VERSUS KEYNESIANISM
M. Townsend: QUANTITY THEORY OF MONEY
John Vaizey: ECONOMICS OF EDUCATION
P. Victor: ECONOMICS OF POLLUTION
J. Wiseman: PRICING PROBLEMS OF THE NATIONALISED INDUSTRIES

Regional Economic Policy

FRANK J. B. STILWELL
Lecturer in Economics, University of Sydney

Macmillan

First published 1972 by
THE MACMILLAN PRESS LTD
London and Basingstoke
Associated companies in New York Toronto
Dublin Melbourne Johannesburg and Madras

SBN 333 13249 1

Printed in Great Britain by
THE ANCHOR PRESS LTD
Tiptree, Essex

Contents

Preface

Regional policy is a pragmatic field of study. We are surrounded in our daily lives by problems of location, and public authorities face recurrent demands concerning the spatial distribution of resources. Sometimes the problems involve the exploitation of opportunities, such as the opening up of a new regional market; sometimes (and more important from a social viewpoint) they involve rectifying existing problems, such as localised unemployment and metropolitan congestion. Either way, an understanding of the spatial aspect of economic systems is a prerequisite for responsible decision-making. This essay deals with some of the most important issues.

I feel that the subject of regional policy requires more attention from academics and policy-makers. Even an elementary understanding of the spatial aspects of a price system reveals systematic tendencies towards non-optimal distribution of resources. The more one studies the subject, the more it becomes apparent that systematic public policy is necessary. Both equity and efficiency considerations demand this intervention in the operations of market economies. The main question is what form such intervention should take.

I am grateful to Professor John Dunning of the University of Reading for stimulating my interest in this field of study, and to Manfred Streit (University of Reading), Tony Thirlwall (University of Kent), Gavan Butler (University of Sydney) and David Pearce (University of Southampton) for their comments on this particular essay. I hope the outcome of it all is to stimulate more discussion, improve the standard of debate and eventually lead to more systematic public policies.

F. J. B. S.

1 The Need for Regional Policy

REGIONAL INEQUALITIES: THE ECONOMIC, POLITICAL AND SOCIAL ISSUES

Regional inequalities exist in many forms: unequal social opportunities (e.g. to see opera or theatre productions, to obtain skilled health services, higher education, or a wide choice of marriage partners), unequal political opportunities (e.g. in the sense of unequal numbers on the electoral roll in different constituencies) and unequal economic opportunities (e.g. to obtain suitable employment, or a real wage equal to that paid for the same job in another area).

Such inequalities are universal but do not of themselves constitute a case for regional policy. It is necessary to ask whether the inequalities constitute *problems* and, if so, whether their solution requires specific *intervention*. The first question can be appraised by reference either to standards of equity or of efficiency. (This important distinction will be used frequently in subsequent analysis; the most general definition of the efficiency concept is in terms of maximising social welfare for a given pattern of income distribution – not necessarily synonymous with measured output, as we shall see later – whereas equity is concerned with the evenness or 'fairness' of the income distribution.) By definition, inequality is a problem if the standards of equity are absolute, but we are usually prepared to condone, or at least disregard, inequalities up to a certain maximum level. The difficulty is in forming a consensus on precisely where that level is. The relationship between inequality and efficiency is even less clear. For example, inequality in regional unemployment levels is normally inconsistent with maximum efficiency of resource use, but there is not *necessarily* any conflict with resource growth efficiency. Thus, inequality and inefficiency are neither necessarily consistent nor inconsistent. To add a further complication, we should note that the efficiency and equity objectives themselves may be in conflict. The ramifications of this are considered later; for the moment it is sufficient to note that this potential conflict means that to consider regional inequalities as a problem by reference either to the efficiency or the equity criterion is inadequate. The establishment of a case for regional policy requires that both be considered.

Even if it can be shown that inequalities constitute a problem, we must demonstrate further that they are not self-correcting before we have a case for intervention. It is necessary to show either that free market forces do not operate to remove the problem or that they do not do so with adequate speed. Thus, the justification for regional policy in predominantly market economies rests to a large measure on the imperfections of the market mechanisms operating in a spatial framework.

However, it does not follow that the appropriate policies should be couched solely in terms of the lubrication of market mechanisms. Political and social objectives may impose severe constraints. For example, consider the policy of reducing regional unemployment differentials by encouraging inter-regional mobility of labour. This is an attempt to frame regional policy in terms of reducing market imperfections, but such a policy may impose social costs in terms of breaking up family units: the dictates of economic efficiency may require that part of a family moves in order to obtain employment. If this is deemed undesirable, it follows that we regard the cohesion of family groups more as an objective than as a regrettable market imperfection! Secondly, consider an alternative means of lubrication: legislation against the process of national wage bargaining. As we shall see later, this allows the market to operate more smoothly by ensuring that regional wage differentials reflect differences in the local demand for and supply of labour. However, it means that employees in some regions will be faced with wage reductions. The social consequences – and their reflection in voting behaviour – may be sufficient to deter a government from such a policy.

It is this interdependence between economic, political and social issues which lends the study of regional economics much of its fascination as well as its complexity. It also results in a very wide range of styles adopted by writers in this field, from mathematical models to political polemics. The fusion of these approaches into a coherent approach to regional policy is the central task facing us.

ALTERNATIVE APPROACHES TO REGIONAL ECONOMIC POLICY

The most ambitious approach to formulating regional economic policy is to regard it as the establishment of the spatial framework for national development. Thus, the government's responsibility is the establishment of such controls, incentives, etc., as are necessary to ensure that the spatial distribution of economic growth develops in accordance with specified objectives of equity and efficiency. It is a matter of ensuring that harmony between equilibrium and optimum states is maintained during the various stages of national growth.

The appropriate emphasis of regional policy varies with the phase of development. Friedmann suggests that there are four such phases: preindustrial, transitional, industrial and post-industrial [60]. Preindustrial societies, such as Burma, Cambodia or Afghanistan, need pay least attention to regional aspects. The emphasis of economic policy at this stage should usually be on improvements in education, health, agricultural organisation and transportation necessary for initiating the process of industrial development. However, once the 'take-off' into industrial growth begins, regional policy becomes crucial. The transition from a rural to an industrial economy requires fundamental changes in spatial organisation, and concentration of industrial developments in growth centres usually results from the attempt to derive the full benefits of external economies. This is what has been termed the *dualistic* structure of developing economies: a centre of rapid intense growth and a periphery whose economy is either stagnant or declining. Examples are to be found in many countries, including Brazil, India, Pakistan, Mexico, Colombia and Venezuela, and Williamson's investigations of regional income levels confirm that regional inequalities are largest in countries at this particular stage of development [64].

The industrial stage is characterised partly by a 'hangover' of the regional problems from the transitional stage, and partly

9

by new difficulties such as the depressed area problem. Thus, the unwillingness or inability to secure a more even regional spread of industry leaves certain areas still relatively under-developed while others suffer because of their overdependence on particular industrial sectors. This is usually regarded as a problem of overspecialisation of industry by region. Examples are to be found in most countries of Western Europe, such as France, West Germany, Italy and the United Kingdom. Finally, in what Friedmann calls postindustrial societies, there are the problems of congestion and urban renewal. Thus, in countries such as the United States, the main emphasis of regional policy turns to urban planning and the conflict between the dictates of private economic efficiency and environmental quality. This is clearly reflected in the nature of regional studies undertaken in the United States: emphasis tends to be on local area problems rather than on the problems of inter-regional resource allocation which characterise much of the European literature. It is not that problems of urban congestion are absent elsewhere so much as that the relative emphasis placed on these problems depends upon the level of economic development attained.

By recognising that the character of the regional problem changes in this fairly predictable sequence, steps can be taken to minimise the difficulties at each stage. Thus, in the transitional stage, care may be taken to avoid the later depressed area problem by ensuring adequate diversification of industry by region. Similarly, in solving depressed area problems it is clearly advisable to avoid those solutions which will add to urban congestion problems at a later stage. This is what is meant by looking at regional policy from the national development viewpoint. The more typical approach is the *ad hoc* solution of regional problems as they arise (and obtain political importance!).

PROBLEM AREAS

It follows from the preceding discussion that there are three main types of problem area: underdeveloped, depressed and congested.

Underdeveloped regions exist in all nations. Even in a

densely populated country like the U.K. there are large areas, particularly in Scotland, Wales and the South-west, which have attracted very little industrial growth. Elsewhere in Europe such regions are even more widespread. The most prominent areas are southern Italy, the west and south-west of France, the north of Sweden, Finland and Norway, much of mainland Denmark and eastern Netherlands. West Germany has several underdeveloped regions such as Schleswig-Holstein, as well as areas near the border with East Germany whose development was curtailed by the severance of their natural market areas.

It does not follow that regional policy should be directed to channelling industry to these regions: they may be inherently unsuited by reason of topological, climatic or other locational factors. A more appropriate solution may be through encouragement to the sectors on which the regional prosperity currently depends, typically agriculture and/or mining and/or tourism. A third alternative is to encourage the further run-down through emigration, so that the region remains relatively underdeveloped, perhaps taking on the function of a national park. However, the very political forces which bring such problem regions into the limelight may act strongly against the adoption of such a solution! From a purely economic viewpoint the choice of policy measures should be based on an evaluation of the long-run viability of the various sectors of the regional economy (both those sectors currently established and those potentially introduced). If only temporary subsidies are required, then the familiar 'infant industry' arguments are applicable. The arguments for long-run subsidies are more difficult to establish and depend largely upon the evaluation of the social costs imposed by continued unemployment and emigration.

The second group of problem regions are also to be found in most developed nations and are an especially common feature in Western Europe. These are areas which have undergone the process of industrialisation, but reveal a poor performance in terms of the usual economic indicators: high unemployment, low activity rates (the proportion of the working-age population in employment or registered as unemployed), low per capita incomes, etc. The root problem is the slow growth of demand (relative to its supply) for labour in such regions.

11

British examples are to be found in South Wales, Merseyside, Yorkshire and Humberside and parts of Scotland and the Northern Region. On the Continent the outstanding examples in the post-war period have been the Ruhr area of Germany (which has improved considerably in the last few years) and Walloon Belgium. To explain the relative stagnation of such regions two hypotheses have been forwarded, locational and structural.

The structural view is the more traditional: that the slow growth results from the unfavourable economic structure of these regions and, in particular, their above-average dependence on industries which are static or declining in demand at the national level. Hence, it is argued, policy should concentrate on counteracting this unfortunate inheritance by measures to 'improve' the industrial mix in the less prosperous regions. The alternative view is that the poor performance in these regions is the result of some endemic disadvantage, such as their peripheral location as regards the major market centres. As a result, modern growth industries will not be attracted to these regions unless these disadvantages can be removed, or at least counterbalanced, by improvements in regional infrastructure, particularly transport links with other regions, and other more direct incentives to industry. McCrone discusses these alternatives more fully and shows that the two hypotheses are not necessarily in direct conflict, in that one region's poor economic performance is often the joint result of both effects [55]. Moreover, the two policies of 'correcting the industrial mix' and 'improving the infrastructure' may be substitutable, at least to a limited extent. Infrastructure improvements may lead to an increased demand for labour in regions with an unfavourable industrial structure, just as regions with locational and other disadvantages may benefit from policies to make their industrial mix more favourable in the light of national trends.

The distinction between locational and structural disadvantage is best regarded as a first step in the disaggregation of depressed area problems. It requires supplementation by more micro-oriented studies of the reasons underlying poor performance by particular industries in particular regions. The whole question of inter-industry and inter-regional linkages must be examined. What is the most appropriate

12

structure for any one region depends on the interrelationships between that region and other areas. Until more is known of these relationships, little can be said about the aggregate impact of particular developments in particular regions. There is no obvious substitute for inter-regional input–output analysis here. A useful introduction to this technique has been provided by Walter Isard, 'the father of regional science' [42]. There are various types of input–output model used in regional analysis, but all involve quantifying the buyer–seller relationships between the various sectors of the regional economy and industries in other regions. This makes it possible to trace through the impact of any change in final demand on the various internal sectors of the region. Thus an input–output table, by describing the existing structure of each region, provides a means of investigating what improvement in economic prosperity can be achieved without fundamental structural changes. The technique suffers from a number of well-known limitations, such as fixed technical and regional coefficients, but does serve to emphasise the importance of treating regions as open rather than closed economies.

The third group of problem regions are those suffering from congestion. It is important to be clear on what is meant by congestion: it is not synonymous with concentration of economic activities in space but refers only to situations where, at the margin, increases in concentration add more to total diseconomies than to total economies. Isard has suggested how the average cost of different urban services (power, education, refuse collection, etc.) will tend to attain its minimum value at different urban sizes and, further, that the per capita cost of providing the whole group of services will tend to fall and then rise with urban scale [17]. This implies that there is an optimum town size from the viewpoint of minimising the cost of providing urban services (depending upon the particular range of services provided). Turning to the demand side, Klaassen has extended the analysis by introducing the effect of urban scale on per capita incomes [61]. It is hypothesised – but not empirically substantiated – that average incomes will rise with urban size, but at a diminishing rate. This means that there must be a level at which the difference between gross income per capita and service costs per capita is maximised (i.e. at OA in Fig. 1).

13

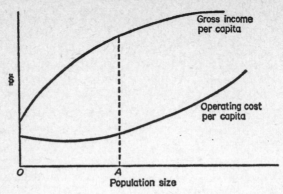

FIG. 1. Economies and diseconomies of urban size

There is no natural tendency for the concentration to attain this value. Since firms and households take their location decisions on the basis of private costs and benefits and have no reason to consider the external effects of their actions, there is no mechanism ensuring harmony between equilibrium and optimum town sizes. The problem for policy formation centres on identifying the level of this optimum, and empirical work to date has been very inconclusive. Neutze's analysis of Australian cities is the most interesting, his tentative conclusion being that cities with a population below 200,000 or above one million are at odds with the requirements of maximum efficiency [20].

The role of regional policy in relation to congested areas is most simply regarded as diverting population growth away from the large centres to new towns and/or expanding small existing towns. The two main problems would seem to be the scale of this redirection and the interdependence between congested and depressed areas. Redirection of population and employment is certainly easier on a local scale, switching new growth out to satellite towns rather than to distant regions. However, its economic effects may be less desirable, because multiplier and other secondary effects of new developments may continue to provide growth pressures for the congested centres. The secondary effects of new developments in distant regions, on the other hand, will assist in the creation of 'counter-magnets' to existing congested centres. The second problem is of the interdependence between congested and depressed regions. Frequently the largest towns of these latter areas are of sufficient size to be considered as congested, e.g. Glasgow, Newcastle, Liverpool. In such cases the region as a whole might need more than its share of new industrial developments while its major cities require decentralisation. There is no necessary conflict here, but it does mean that co-ordination is necessary between depressed region policies and more localised land-use planning policies; otherwise the problem of congestion may not be reduced so much as relocated.

THE ROLE OF GOVERNMENT

The case for intervention stems from the inadequacy of free market forces. In an 'ideal' economic world, free market forces correct all spatial imbalances through the price mechanism. Where resources are relatively scarce, their prices rise and, as a result, demand falls and supply rises. Conversely, where resources are underutilised, their prices fall, leading to an increase in demand and a decrease in supply. The process continues until equilibrium is attained in all markets. How, then, can intervention be justified? Partly because this 'ideal' world does not adequately describe the real world, and partly because, even if it did, we should not regard it as 'ideal' in the normative sense.

First, there are reasons why factor prices do not reflect relative scarcities in different regions. The process of national wage bargaining, for example, can lead to a situation where the price of a particular type of labour can rise in a region where it is in excess supply. This is the result of successful wage claims being transmitted from other regions where the same occupational group is facing an excess demand. Secondly, even if relative scarcities are reflected in factor prices, it does not follow that factors will move freely from areas where the price offered is low to areas where the price offered is high. There are many social and psychological barriers to inter-regional migration. One has already been mentioned: the unwillingness to break up a family unit where migration would involve only part of a household. In such circumstances, free market forces will not remove regional unemployment differentials. Thirdly, there is the obvious point that, even if market forces were equilibrating in the long run, the interim period of adjustment might be regarded as unnecessarily painful. As Nevin notes, policy can seldom allow its horizons to extend into infinity [5]. In the long run – to quote the one piece of Keynes which *every* student gets right – we are all dead.

Having established a prima facie case for intervention, it is necessary to specify the objectives sought. A brief, and admittedly crude, classification of national economic objectives is appropriate here. The widely used distinction between resource utilisation, allocation and growth suggests the following primary considerations:

(i) prevention of resource underutilisation;
(ii) securing optimal allocation of resources between sectors;
(iii) achievement of a satisfactory rate of resource growth.

The first of these is the most widely accepted, especially in relation to the unemployment of labour resources. The second two objectives require more elaboration. Nourse lists the three main causes of divergence from optimality as externalities, monopoly, and goods not being subject to the exclusion principle [22].[1] This whole question of necessary and sufficient conditions for allocative efficiency is a complex one from the theoretical viewpoint. The most general statement that can be made is that where there is a demonstrable divergence from optimality, then the government has a responsibility for correcting the resource misallocation. Point (iii) requires a statement of what constitutes a satisfactory growth rate. This is not necessarily synonymous with the maximum attainable: Mishan has clearly demonstrated how the pursuit of the maximum has undesirable repercussions on resource allocation and on non-economic goals [18].

The list can be extended by explicit reference to other commonly cited government objectives:

(iv) prevention of excessive inflation;
(v) avoidance of persistent balance of payments disequilibria.

Fundamentally, these are means to the fulfilment of the first three objectives: a high rate of inflation tends to cause a persistent balance of payments deficit, which leads in turn to

[1] For a fuller reference to the significance of the exclusion principle see M. Peston, *Public Goods and the Public Sector*, Studies in Economics (Macmillan, London, forthcoming).

unemployment via the familiar deflationary internal economic policies. This also will tend to lower the attainable rate of economic growth which, given continuing population pressure, may further add to the unemployment problem. It is because these inflation and payments balance objectives are secondary from the economic efficiency viewpoint that there is less need to specify precisely what is meant by 'excessive' inflation or 'persistent' balance of payments disequilibria. This is important for establishing short-term targets, but in the long run what is acceptable depends on the relationship with more fundamental objectives.

Turning from efficiency to equity objectives, we can add the Government's responsibility regarding:

    (vi) establishment of reasonable equity in the distribution of income.

Of course, there is no clear consensus on what is meant by 'reasonable' in this context. Moreover, this equity objective is interrelated with efficiency considerations; for example, inflation is one cause of inequity in that it makes relatively worse off those groups of society living off fixed incomes, notably pensioners. Also, equity is related to growth via the incentive offered to effort, although the correlation may be either positive or negative depending on the relative values of the income and substitution effects in the income–leisure choice.

Regional policy can be regarded as the application of a spatial framework in the achievement of these objectives. Its potential contribution is twofold: direct influence on each of the specified national policy objectives, and in reducing the incompatibility of the individual objectives. The clearest role is in the prevention of resource underutilisation: the reduction of unemployment (including involuntary unemployment concealed in low activity rates) where it is most concentrated. As far as resource allocation is concerned, we have already noted some of the externalities and market imperfections associated with locational choice. Regional policy can help to correct the resulting tendencies to suboptimal allocation of resources. There is also a potential contribution to the achievement of satisfactory growth, over and above the once-and-for-all impact of reducing localised unemployment. This is because imbalance in the regional labour market may act as a constraint on growth in that it

17

tends to cause a higher rate of inflation than the overall level of aggregate demand would otherwise dictate. The role of regional policy in relation to balance of payments disequilibria is less clear, unless the policy is especially designed to make more buoyant those regions specialising in the production of exports and/or import substitutes. More generally, since national balance of payments difficulties are often thought to result from labour market disequilibria of various types, regional policy has a role to play via its effects on the efficiency with which the labour market operates. Finally, regional policy offers an obvious contribution in relation to equity objectives of national policy. Inter-regional inequalities in post-tax income per capita could be reduced by greater progression in national tax rates, but their removal requires either a national taxation policy designed to equate all post-tax incomes or some specific policies with a spatial dimension.

2 Objectives of Regional Policy

SPECIFYING MEASURABLE GOALS

Much discussion of regional policy is couched in terms of 'promoting sound growth in the regions', securing 'a proper distribution of industry', 'regional balance', or diverting to the less prosperous regions 'a fair share' of national economic growth. The looseness of this terminology often reflects an unwillingness to specify the precise objectives of regional policy. The result is that it becomes very difficult to evaluate the success of policies when the objectives sought are so vaguely stated. The political advantages of such a procedure are well known, but for the purpose of applying economic analysis a more specific statement of aims is fundamental.

An economic decision model is one in which instrumental or policy variables are related together with other independent variables to specified targets. In a multiple regression approach, for example, the policy variables are set so as to bring into equality the predicted and desired values of the endogenous variable, given the predicted values of the other exogenous variables. Clearly it is essential to deal with quantifiable objectives.

Perloff has suggested a catalogue of various measures of regional progress [6]. The following list of welfare (or standard of living) indices derives from his suggestion:

(i) measures of the proportion of the labour force (actively seeking work) who are employed;
(ii) measures of the material state or condition of individuals;
(iii) measures of per capita consumption of goods and services;
(iv) measures of per capita income.

The first of these is peculiar in that it helps only in the identification of persons with low welfare and tells us nothing about

19

the welfare of the rest of the regional population. Also, its effects will be reflected in the other indices. The second type of index is more general and there are a number of possibilities here, ranging from personal standards of health, education, etc., to housing values and conditions (e.g. percentage of homes having inside toilet, hot-water tap, etc.). The third index could be identified either through information on retail turnover or, in a more restricted way, through information on ownership of consumers' durables. The fourth is the most commonly used welfare index (in developed countries at least) and is certainly the most general. Unlike the previous two indices, mean income levels by region do not directly reflect inter-regional differences in preference functions. The main complications are the measurement of incomes in underdeveloped regions and the problem of trying to take account of features of the income distribution other than the mean. Regional progress may be viewed in terms of achieving a more equitable distribution of income within the region as well as a higher mean level, in which case it is necessary to construct a composite index of progress reflecting the normative trade-off between mean income levels and equality in the distribution.

Perloff's further suggestion that regional progress can be measured in terms of efficiency and volume is less acceptable. From the efficiency viewpoint, progress would involve an increasing ratio of regional value added to the inputs of capital and labour; from the volume viewpoint, it would involve simply the growth of regional output or inputs. However, such efficiency and volume considerations are ultimately relevant only to the extent to which they bear on welfare. Hence, direct measurement of progress in terms of welfare indices is preferable, unless it can be demonstrated that these efficiency and volume indices provide early-warning signals of changes which take time to have a final impact on regional prosperity.

The choice between alternative welfare indices is not simple, but the greater the formality of the economic approach applied, the more important it becomes to have unique and quantifiable yardsticks of progress. It is true that the indices are correlated in most instances, e.g. regions in which housing standards are poor also tend to be characterised by low per capita income and consumption levels and by above-average unemployment. However, these correlations are seldom perfect and the application of formal models requires that some choice be made (or that specific weighting to the various indices be given in the formation of a composite index). Then the vague objectives mentioned earlier can be refined and interpreted in these less ambiguous terms. Thus, a 'fair share' of national growth may be viewed as the increase in national income multiplied by the proportion of national population living within the region in question, or as that proportion of new industrial development needed in order to reduce the regional unemployment percentage to the national average.

To make the further step of translating these regional policy objectives into specific planning targets requires a statement of the rate of regional equalisation sought. In practice, complete equality is seldom cited even as a long-term goal: the target is more likely to be set in a form such as 'a 20 per cent reduction within ten years in the absolute difference between per capita incomes in the prosperous and the less prosperous regional groupings'. Even then constraints are likely to be set: for example, that such equalisation must not take place by reducing mean income levels in the prosperous regional group, i.e. that the equalisation must occur through a reallocation of net growth rather than through a transfer of existing incomes. It is to these important interrelationships between regional and national objectives that we now turn.

CONFLICTS BETWEEN OBJECTIVES

National and regional objectives are often strongly interrelated. Thus, a regional policy may be pursued to achieve national objectives as listed earlier, such as raising national economic growth by reducing the amount of inflation associated with a given national unemployment level. On the other hand, the objectives of national (and international) economic policy always have either an explicit or implicit regional dimension. A policy in which the spatial dimension is explicit would be one of offering financial incentives to businessmen to locate their firms in particular geographical areas. However, spatial dimensions may also be implicit in other policies, such as a general increase in unemployment benefits or the progressiveness of the income-tax structure. Both these policies would normally increase the relative prosperity of the least prosperous regions. In other cases, such as tariff policies or quota restrictions on imports, the impact on different regions is less easy to determine. The effect may be either to widen or narrow regional income differentials, depending, *inter alia*, on the regional distribution of industry and on inter-regional linkages.

It is this implicit spatial aspect of national policy decisions that underlies the potential conflict between national and regional economic objectives. Consider a government deciding on its allocation of investment between industrial sectors and regions. It can follow either of two allocation procedures:

(i) select the regional distribution of the investment according to explicit regional objectives, and then decide on the sector in which the investment should take place; or

(ii) select the sectoral distribution of investment according to some national objective, and then decide on the regional distribution.

The resulting allocation may be quite different. For example, the decision in the latter case may be to invest in the iron and steel industry, but if the least prosperous region has a comparative disadvantage in steel production, it will not obtain the share of government investment that it would have received in the former case.

Only by integrating the sectoral and regional decisions into a simultaneous decision model can the conflicts between regional and national objectives be resolved. The problems involved here have been considered by Isard and Reiner [1] and other authors in the same volume. One fruitful solution demonstrated by Leven [2] and Reiner [7] is the application of linear programming techniques. Thus, we might regard the national objective as a constraint on the achievement of the regional objective. More probably, we would regard the national objective as primary and the regional objective as a constraint on its achievement. Thus we might seek to maximise the rate of growth of GNP subject to the condition that income in the poorest region does not fall relative to the national average. Thus, in a two-region economy, with total regional incomes Y_a and Y_b (Y_b being the lower) and growth rates p_a and p_b, we would seek to maximise $\Upsilon p = (\Upsilon_a p_a + \Upsilon_b p_b)$ subject to the constraint that $p_b \geqslant p_a$. This constraint may or may not affect the solution. As a general rule, the regional objective is operative only when its effect is in opposition to the regional effects implicit in policy decisions based on national objectives. This means that there will be a conflict between regional and national objectives only when the least prosperous region has a comparative disadvantage in the sector most productive from the national growth viewpoint. In the earlier example, the poorest region had a comparative disadvantage in iron and steel; had it had a comparative advantage in this sector, there would have been no conflict between the regional and national objectives. Then the allocation of investment would have been the same if either the national or the regional objectives had been ignored.

The major alternative to resolution of conflicts between national and regional objectives through linear programming is provided by the direct specification of efficiency–equity trade-offs. All national policy decisions involve equity as well as efficiency considerations: as we saw earlier, the income distribution objective is interrelated with the other government objectives. Since there is a potential conflict – some policies may increase national growth but cause a less favourable income distribution, while policies of increasing equity in distribution may restrict growth – some trade-off must be applied. Indeed, these trade-offs are always present either in an explicit or implicit form; they cannot be eliminated by ignoring them.

In the regional context, the trade-off can usually be considered as that between inter-regional equity and aggregate efficiency. Regional policies do not necessarily have a cost in terms of aggregate efficiency, but may do so in certain cases; and it is in these circumstances that we need to know the cost of pursuing the regional objective in terms of the violence done to the national objective. Mera has shown how Edgeworth box analysis can be used in the derivation of transformation surfaces between efficiency and equity, once the regional production functions are known [4]. Then the cost of efficiency in terms of equity can be seen to vary with the rate of factor substitution possible. The closer the production functions approximate to the fixed-coefficient type (and the further they deviate from the Cobb–Douglas type), the lower is the cost of one objective in terms of the other. This analysis is based on very severe assumptions, and its contribution is largely in demonstrating that, conceptually at least, it is possible to relate the values of efficiency–equity trade-offs to particular regional characteristics.

In practice, trade-offs between inter-regional equity and aggregate efficiency are involved in a variety of decisions. The classic case is that of a central agency distributing funds between localised projects, some of which have high efficiency ratings but are located in prosperous regions, and some of which are less efficient but located in poor regions in greater need of the boost to the local economy. Only if a trade-off between efficiency and equity is specified – say, 1 per cent of aggregate economic growth per 5 per cent reduction in a concentration ratio describing the inter-regional distribution of income – can rational and consistent choices be made by the central agency.

The value of the trade-offs is seldom made explicit, but can be identified by analysis of past decisions. The study by McGuire and Garn [3] is particularly interesting in revealing the lack of consistency in decision-making. There are some causes of inconsistency which may be justifiable (e.g. the need to consider non-quantifiable factors which cannot be expressed in simple efficiency and equity indices) but others which are not (e.g. the tendency of decisions taken by groups to be inconsistent and the tendency of individuals to be inconsistent because of doubts about their own judgement). A quantified efficiency–equity trade-off can help to improve the resource allocation between regions by reducing the incidence of these latter cases.

3 Contributions of Regional Economic Theory

SPATIAL MICRO-ECONOMICS

The potential contribution of micro-economics to the framing of regional policy lies in the fuller understanding of the factors influencing individual location decisions. Most weapons of regional policy in mixed economies are directed towards influencing these individual decisions: hence, greater knowledge of the preference functions enables the selection of policy instruments to be more scientific.

The set of location decisions which has attracted most attention from regional scientists is that of the firm. Theories of firm location can be grouped into four categories according to the motivation attributed to the entrepreneur (or group of persons) taking the location decisions. These are: (i) minimising costs, (ii) maximising revenue, (iii) maximising profit, and (iv) satisficing.

The problem of selecting a site at which a given product can be produced at minimum cost has inspired a number of models emphasising the cost of transporting inputs and outputs. Isard provides a useful summary, and demonstrates further how transport can itself be regarded as an input into the productive process, such that the locational choice of the firm is analogous to the choice of factor combinations [17]. Thus, the firm is seen as selecting a location by trading off distance from raw materials and market against advantages in terms of reduced costs of labour, power, etc. It is then possible to superimpose the effects on location of agglomeration economies and diseconomies. These can be classified into effects internal to the firm (economies and diseconomies of scale), to the particular industry (economies and diseconomies of concentration) and to all industries (economies and diseconomies of urbanisation). All these will affect the private

25

cost of producing a given output at alternative sites. Three things should be clear about these least-cost theories of location. First, there is no mention of the *social* costs of selecting alternative locations: there is no reason why the private firm should consider these unless there are specific policies in force which mean that these social costs become (via taxes, compensation payments, subsidies, etc.) reflected in private costs. Secondly, the decision-maker is assumed to have perfect knowledge of costs in different locations. Thirdly, the least-cost location analysis is consistent with profit maximisation only if the total revenue of the firm is invariant with location.

Maximum revenue theories of firm location as developed from the early contributions of Hotelling [16] and Smithies [25] start from an opposite assumption – that location determines revenues rather than costs. Given the spatial distribution of the market, the principal influence on site selection is the location of competitive firms. This tends to cause systematic deviations from minimum-cost locations, especially because of incentives to agglomeration. The main feature of this group of theories is an inherent problem of instability, and the application of game theory appears a potentially fruitful means of handling these situations. Further developments may also arise from the recognition of locational interdependence between complementary (as well as competing) activities. Distance from complementary firms may affect either costs or revenues depending on whether the relationship is one of supplier or consumer and how inter-company transportation costs are charged. However, only the influence on revenue can strictly be integrated into the maximum-revenue theories of location since it is necessary to assume costs independent of location. The maximum-revenue theories of location are similar to the least-cost theories in that they ignore social costs. Indeed, one of the persistent themes of contributors in this field is the systematic tendency to non-optimal situations which results from locational interdependence. Also, the assumption of perfect knowledge of location alternatives appears once again.

The third main type of location theory attempts to investigate the effects of variation in both costs and revenues with respect to location. Greenhut has provided a useful synthesis of least-cost and maximum-revenue approaches and usefully emphasises the importance of making both cost and revenue calculations in site selection [15].

The formal condition for profit maximisation is that each producer will select the location from which its sales to a given number of buyers (whose purchases are needed for maximum profits) can be supplied at the lowest total costs. Clearly, this will normally involve some compromise between minimum-cost and maximum-revenue sites. The cost-minimising and revenue-maximising models then become special cases of a more general model. The question remains as to what policy recommendations are thrown up by this approach to studying industrial location. The two most obvious are:

(i) to develop a system of taxes and incentives which makes the individual firm's profit-maximising location synonymous with the social optimum;

(ii) to assist location decision-makers to perfect their knowledge of both costs and revenues in alternative sites.

These implications for policy depend upon the assumption that businessmen seek to maximise their profits. Whether this is a useful approximation to the general goal of business behaviour is an apparently endless controversy; but even if profit maximisation provides a useful basis for models of price, output and investment decisions, it appears less suitable for location decisions. Chance and 'the early start' have long been recognised as important location influences, but recent empirical research suggests that there are some relatively systematic characteristics of firms' location decision-making. The evidence of Law [52], Loasby [53], Needleman and Scott [32] and others suggests that the typical process has the following features:

(i) The location decision arises as the result of a near-crisis situation, such that a speedy decision is more important than an ideal decision.

(ii) There is no systematic consideration of costs and revenues in alternative sites. After conducting a thorough survey of manufacturing location in Britain, Luttrell was able to conclude: 'We should have liked to give an example of the classic location choice in which operating cost estimates were made for two or more possible places, all imponderables or non-cost factors assessed and then a way found of comparing the good and bad points of one place with those of the other. Unfortunately, we have not been able to find such a case' [54].

(iii) The tendency is to seek something suitable close at hand, the implicit assumption being that the present location is probably optimal. The firm thereby searches outwards and accepts the nearest site which appears satisfactory.

This is what forms the framework of the newly-emerging 'satisficing' theory of locational selection. Like the more general behavioural theories of the firm, emphasis is placed on the reluctance to undertake search procedures and on the achievement of minimum rather than maximum objectives. A general theory of satisficing behaviour in location choice has yet to be developed, but exploratory efforts suggest that attempts to place a pecuniary value on the non-monetary objectives involved in locational choice are unlikely to lead to satisfactory results. The essence of modern organisation theory is that decisions evolve out of group processes and do not directly reflect any identifiable or stable objective function. Hence, by making the theory of firm location more 'realistic', we increase our understanding at the expense of a sacrifice in predictive power. However, the sacrifice is profitable in this particular case because this explicit recognition of the typically non-maximising nature of locational selection has several important implications for regional policy:

(i) That locational selection is potentially amenable to a considerable amount of influence without necessarily any sacrifice of private efficiency. Interference might lead either to an efficiency loss or an efficiency gain depending on whether the site freely selected by the firm would turn out to be a lower- or higher-cost location than the one to which the government steers it.

(ii) The instruments of regional policy need not necessarily be designed precisely in terms of the externalities of locational choice. Cruder instruments, such as administrative controls, may be more effective in dealing with firms who do not respond to monetary incentives like traditional profit-maximisers.

(iii) As emphasised by Cable, simplicity and conspicuousness should be the order of the day [48]. Simple policy instruments are likely to have more influence than sophisticated ones even though their monetary value to the firm be smaller.

Theories of household location have much in common with those of firm location. Of course, there is strong interdependence: firm location is influenced by household distribution because of labour availability and 'distance to market' considerations, while household location is influenced by firm location via labour market considerations. This interrelationship with the location of industry is the outstanding characteristic of household location models. Alonso's study is a good example [13]. It offers valuable insights into the systematic forces in the development of land-use patterns and urban form, but provides relatively little direct guidance for the formulation of inter-regional policies. There is some consideration of the effects of zoning on land use, but the main concern is with equilibrium rather than optimum outcomes. Emphasis on the latter turns attention again to the effect of externalities. As with industry, there is no reason to expect any tendency towards optimality in the spatial distribution of households. There is the similar point that housing costs do not necessarily reflect the social costs of such development: the mere fact that new house builders are not usually required to compensate existing residents of an area for their loss of amenity suggests a natural tendency to excessive density levels. Moreover, given the interdependence between residential and industrial location and the non-optimality of industrial location, there will be consistent tendencies towards non-optimality in residential location.

The other main strand of household location theory relates to the migration process itself. The earliest models leaned strongly on physical analogies, and these are well summarised by Isard [42]. Gravity models in particular have formed the basis of a number of intra-urban residential location studies in the United States. These models view population size as the attractive (or gravitational) pull between two places, and intervening distance (or sometimes intervening job opportunities) as the element causing friction. Depending on the values of the coefficients relating these variables to migration, the movement of persons between any two places can be predicted. However, this approach yields very little in terms of policy implications because its role is to provide statistical approximations rather than behavioural insights. Current research in developing migration models from individual utility analysis involving conditions of uncertainty seems likely to be more fruitful. However, to date the main contribution of economic theory in this area centres not so much on the causes of labour mobility as on the economic consequences of such movement. In particular, there is the important question of whether labour migration has equilibrating or disequilibrating effects – for more on which see Section 4 below.

SPATIAL MACRO-ECONOMICS

Whereas spatial micro-economics does not assume any regional boundaries and looks at individual location decisions in terms of a continuous space variable, spatial macro-economics must assume some regional framework to which macro-theories of growth and development can be applied.

It is convenient to group the various theories of regional growth as follows:
  (i) those that consider growth to arise as a result of resource reallocation;
  (ii) those relating growth to the expansion of the region's export base;
  (iii) those that concentrate upon investment in its relation with the growth of capacity; and
  (iv) those that consider growth as a cumulative process.

Within the first group, two subcategories are identifiable: *intra*-regional reallocation models and *inter*-regional reallocation models. Both rest upon factor mobility as the mechanism producing differences between regions in the rate of economic growth (measured usually in terms of per capita incomes). The first suggests that the rate of growth will be fastest in those areas where the internal misallocation of resources is the greatest (if population growth is everywhere the same). Such misallocation is corrected by resources moving from sectors offering below-average returns to those offering above-average returns. Historically, this has usually meant that rapid economic growth occurs as a result of factors moving from primary to secondary and tertiary industries. This would usually imply convergence in the relative prosperity of different regions:

the most rapid growth will occur in the most 'backward' areas simply because they have the greatest scope for internal resource reallocation.

Inter-regional reallocation models similarly view growth as a process towards an equilibrium situation. These are the best known of all regional growth models, and are usually couched in terms of the familiar neo-classical assumptions of full employment, perfect mobility of all factors, perfect competition and constant returns to scale. It follows directly from these assumptions that a set of regional economies will be in equilibrium only when factor-price/productivity ratios are identical in all regions. Factors will flow from regions where their prices are low to regions where their prices are high and, on the assumption of diminishing marginal productivity, this will produce an inter-regional equality in the ratio of factor prices to marginal physical productivities. Thus, factor outflows would normally be associated with rising per capita incomes, albeit with falling total regional income.

The policy implications of these models are relatively clear: if the government is seeking to reduce inter-regional differentials in economic prosperity, the appropriate course of action is to institute the assumptions of neo-classical economics! In particular, attention should be concentrated on increasing resource mobility, and hence accelerating the equalisation process. The intra-regional resource reallocation theory would suggest that emphasis be placed on increasing the mobility of factors as between industry and occupations; the inter-regional resource reallocation theory would suggest that emphasis be placed on increasing the mobility of factors geographically.

A second main approach to regional growth stems from emphasising the propulsive effect of regional exports on regional income. Insights into what such models can achieve are provided by the published discussion between North and Tiebout [21, 26]. The concept of the economic base has a long history in urban planning and, when applied at the regional level, suggests that the key to growth lies in understanding the role of exports, i.e. exports from the region either to other regions of the same country or to other countries. In the short run export expansion leads to increases in regional income both directly and via secondary effects on the demand for locally produced goods and services. In the long run there will be changes in the structure of the regional economy resulting from capital and labour movements, and these will tend to reinforce the process of regional growth. It is possible to refine the model so as to identify what particular types of export expansion will have the largest growth effects, but the theory retains crudities which limit its value. Richardson parades an impressive list of drawbacks, perhaps the most important of which is the neglect of internal stimuli, particularly those associated with technological progress, and of exogenous variables other than investment, especially government injections [23]. Nevertheless, the ability of regions to develop industrial structures conducive to the development of exports is widely held to be an important determinant of their growth prospects.

Once again the implications for regional policy are quite clear. Any measures to stimulate the export performance of the least prosperous regions should provide the impetus for the movement towards equalisation of regional prosperity. Export subsidies are the most obvious weapon, but any other instruments forcing down input prices, such as labour or capital subsidies, will have effects in the desired direction if they result in lower prices for final outputs. The main problem would seem to be with regions, especially primary producing areas, facing inelastic demand for their exports. Such regions need to make the transition to more balanced industrial economies before they can benefit fully from measures designed to raise prosperity by direct stimuli to exports. In this case the appropriate role of the government is more in terms of encouraging change in internal structures rather than in terms of giving direct encouragement to regional exports.

A third main approach to regional growth is through the application of national growth models. The best known are the Harrod–Domar models, the application of which to a regional setting owes much to Richardson [23]. This sort of approach concentrates more on the supply variables, and views regional growth as a function of capital accumulation, increases in labour availability and technical progress. The prime source of these increases in supply is through migratory flows. However, these flows do not form an equilibrating mechanism within the models themselves, and divergences from the equilibrium growth path will normally lead to divergent regional growth paths. This is because any lagging in the growth of a region's income will lead to a below-trend value of imports, and it follows from these models that regions with net import surpluses will grow faster than other regions.

The implications for regional policy relate mainly to the level of investment and technical progress in the lagging regions. Once divergent growth paths develop, it is the responsibility of the government to secure a return to the equilibrium path. The most obvious instruments are those operating directly on the regional investment. The regions with the slowest growth rate will be those in which the growth of investment has fallen behind growth of capacity; their prospects for increasing their rate of growth lie in increased investment. The usual two alternatives exist: either direct government investment in the areas in question, or measures to stimulate private investment through incentives to expand output and/or engage in factor substitution. However, the technology embodied in the investment is also of importance. For the nation, the rate of technical progress is important in determining the growth of capacity; for each region, the rate of adoption of technical progress is important in determining whether it lags behind or keeps pace with growth elsewhere.

The final group of theories of regional economic growth are characterised by their dependence on the process of cumulative causation. The classic exposition is that of Myrdal, who considers the less developed regions sometimes in a national framework and sometimes in an international framework (in which case the term 'less developed regions' applies to the most underdeveloped countries) [19]. The general hypothesis is that growth centres, having developed for an assortment of historical/geographical reasons, develop cumulative advantages so that the gap between their prosperity and that of the periphery tends to widen. Among the most frequently cited causes of this divergence are the inadequate and selective nature of migratory flows, the private economies of location in urban centres, and the inability (or unwillingness) of businessmen to perceive economic opportunities in the periphery. So long as these 'backwash' effects dominate the 'spread' effects of development from the centre, then divergent growth trends will result.

This cumulative causation approach to regional growth is of central importance. It seeks to synthesise many elements of the other theories together with additional aspects affecting regional development. As such it is more powerful, and is capable of giving many insights into growth processes. However, the difficulty in drawing policy implications from studies of this sort is that policies are themselves seen as part of the process of cumulative causation. Myrdal suggests that welfare state policies and other means of increasing internal equalities are not developed in poor nations because of the less egalitarian bias in their political systems (reflecting, among other things, the prevalence in poor countries of built-in feudal-type power structures which aid the rich in exploiting the poor). Also, in poorer nations the centralised resources are frequently inadequate to meet the cost of such redistribution.

However, given that the government is not completely impotent in this respect, there are two major alternatives. One is to establish new growth centres in the peripheral regions and channel in as much infrastructure investment as possible, with the intention of counteracting the pull of existing centres. The other is to investigate the nature of individual 'backwash' and 'spread' effects, in order to see how the former may be curtailed and the latter encouraged. One particularly obvious possibility arises from what Friedmann calls 'the failure to perceive peripheral investment opportunities' [60]. The government has a role in counteracting this centralising effect through publicity of such opportunities. Similarly, the relative attraction of the periphery to secondary industry can be increased by policies to effect decentralisation of tertiary services (finance, research and services of all kinds, including those of the national government). Also, of course, the prospects of the periphery can be improved by introducing policies to make firms pay the cost of the external diseconomies generated by their preference for centralised locations. Such policies may help to counteract the widening of regional differentials, although it may be only in the more prosperous countries that the political structure is conducive to their implementation.

So much for the policies suggested by the major strands of regional *growth* theory. The other major aspect of spatial macro-economics relates to *stability*. There are two points of interest: the stability of individual regions and the potential contribution of regional policies to the stability of the national economy.

34

The former has received more attention, particularly in relation to the old industrial areas which are subject to large fluctuations in prosperity because of their dependence on a narrow range of industries. The two policies usually suggested are the diversification of industry and the application of fiscal stabilisation measures. One problem with the diversification approach is the sacrifice of the advantages of regional specialisation. Moreover, there is some evidence to suggest that it is unlikely to be fully effective since only part of the regional variation in amplitude of cycles can be 'explained' by the structure of industry (see Harris and Thirlwall [31]).

Fiscal policies have a more immediate impact on instability. There is a built-in stabilisation effect so long as tax rates are progressive and the rate of expenditure on welfare payments, etc., negatively related to income. In regions prone to cyclical instability, tax payments and receipts of government expenditure fluctuate more than in stable regions, and this has an offsetting effect on the amplitude of fluctuations. The greater the progression in the tax and expenditure schedules (and the smaller the leakages through the marginal propensity to import), the greater the stability. Additionally, the government can use fiscal policy in regional stabilisation by introducing inter-regional variation in the progression of the tax structure. This policy has not been widely used, but similar effects can be achieved by the use of inter-regional variations in monetary policy. Belgium has used cheap finance policies extensively in encouraging development in the Walloon area; even in the U.K. the government has directed the joint-stock banks to pay attention to the aims of regional policy in dealing with applications for finance.

It should be emphasised that it is implicit in this discussion of regional stabilisation that the responsibility for the stability of individual regions lies with central rather than with local governments. Richardson argues this point strongly: that while local authorities can increase stability through surplus and deficit financing, the responsibility for co-ordinating and assessing the impact of localised programmes on aggregate demand must lie with the central authority [23]. To argue, as some central governments have done, that in periods of national economic difficulties local authorities must rely more on internal finance, is clearly at odds with this.

The potential contribution of regional policies to *national* stabilisation has only recently been recognised. One of the central issues is most clearly explained in terms of Phillips curves, showing the relationship between the rate of change in money wages and the percentage level of unemployment.[1] This relation is not so unusual as is sometimes implied, particularly because it may be possible to devise policies to shift the position of the curve. Recent experience of 'stagflation' (quite high levels of unemployment associated with rapid inflationary pressures) in many countries suggests a tendency for the curve to shift to the right. Any policy which could counteract this would enable the economy to be run at lower levels of unemployment and/or inflation. Regional policy is one such possibility. The evidence of Thirlwall [35] and Archibald [27] for the U.K. suggests that in some regions the rate of inflation associated with given levels of unemployment is higher than in others. Moreover, the change in the rate of inflation associated with a given change in unemployment tends to be greater in the regions with low unemployment than in those with high unemployment (i.e. the Phillips curves are steeper in the former case). It follows that an increase in unemployment in the latter regions and a corresponding reduction in the former regions will enable the national economy to be run with a lower rate of inflation. Alternatively, given the national rate of inflation, aggregate unemployment can be reduced through a regional allocation of the demand for and/or supply of labour. In this way, regional policy can reduce the conflict between national economic objectives. Essentially, it means that regional policy takes the form of applying the Keynesian approach at the regional level. Aggregate supply and demand are managed for individual regions, and policies to ensure greater demand–supply harmony at that level provide greater scope for the attainment of objectives at the national level. There are alternative means of achieving the same ends (such as repealing minimum-wage legislation and preventing national wage-bargaining agreements), but this approach to regional policy does less violence to more widely defined social objectives.

[1] For further discussion of Phillips curves, reference should be made to J. Burton, *Wage Inflation*, Studies in Economics (Macmillan, London, 1972).

4 The Strategy of Regional Policy

REGIONAL DELINEATION

Defining the areas to which different regional policies should apply is a fundamental aspect of strategy. Much of the current discussion of policy alternatives in Western Europe relates to this question, in particular to the alternatives of broadly defined development regions and narrowly defined growth points. To understand the debate requires examination of the theoretical possibilities of regional delineation.

The literature on regionalisation methods is quite considerable: Harris, for example, lists 291 references on this subject [41]. Nevertheless, the variety of methods in defining regions can usefully be condensed according to their underlying concept of what constitutes a region. Three such concepts can be identified: those of a region as a homogeneous spatial unit, as a polarised unit and as a programming unit. The last of these has the least theoretical underpinning. What it says is that regions should be defined in terms of the areas under the jurisdiction of the bodies responsible for implementing the regional policy. This is a very pragmatic approach and apparently denies the possibility that the existing administrative boundaries are unsuited to the enactment of regional policy. It is true that the practical difficulties of modifying existing administrative structures may make the programming approach to regional delineation expedient, but if we are interested in optimality rather than expediency we must concentrate on the homogeneity and polarisation concepts of a region.

The homogeneity approach requires that the particular definition of regions be sought which minimises intra-regional variation in the variable (or variables) studied and maximises inter-regional variation. There are three central problems: the choice of the number of separate regional groupings,

37

the selection of the variable (or variables) in terms of which regional homogeneity is to be maximised, and the introduction of constraints on contiguity.

The problem of selecting the number of regions must be resolved by reference to the objectives of policy and, in particular, to its intended sophistication. At one extreme is the proposal of Clark for regional groupings in the U.K.: a series of fine gradations from London, which he argues should be heavily penalised through payroll taxes, to peripheral areas such as the Hebrides, which should receive enormous benefits [30]. Actual policy in the U.K. has tended towards the other extreme, dividing the country into two, Development Areas and the rest. The 1960s saw the introduction of two more categories: Special Development Areas (receiving additional assistance) and Intermediate Areas (receiving less assistance than the Development Areas), and this can be interpreted as a move towards the more sophisticated French regional classification. France has a fivefold division as the basis for its system of locational disincentives and incentives, with the congested Paris area at one extreme and the underdeveloped areas of the north-west, south and south-west at the other. Other European countries are tending to move towards this sort of policy by the introduction of new policies for areas with regional problems intermediate between the favoured and non-favoured regions. It is true that many of the arguments for the introduction of Intermediate Areas in the U.K. were couched in terms of *ad hoc* issues (e.g. the problem of areas just outside the Development Areas in attracting new industrial development, the overspecialised industrial structure of some of these 'grey areas', and so on; see the Hunt Report [57]). However, a more general justification is provided by the earlier discussion of the micro-economics of locational choice. The social costs of congestion and resource misallocation change continuously in space. The finer the gradation of regions for policy purposes, the greater the possibility of minimising the distinction between actual and optimal tax and subsidy levels at each location.

The selection of a variable (or variables) in terms of which regional homogeneity is to be maximised should be related to the objectives of policy. The methodology of regression analysis can be used to explain some of the possibilities. Suppose our regional policy objectives are couched in terms of equalisation of per capita incomes (Y). We further postulate that incomes are functionally related to industrial composition (C) and the extent of urbanisation (R), i.e. $Y = f(C,R)$. Now consider two adjoining counties $(a$ and $b)$: the question is whether they belong in the same or in different regions. There are three possible methods of making the classification:

(i) To classify a and b into the same region if the actual values of the endogenous variable are similar, i.e. if $Y_a - Y_b$ is small. (What constitutes small can be determined by variance analysis: the null hypothesis that there is no significant difference between the two areas is tested for a specified level of probability.)

(ii) To classify a and b into the same region if the estimated values of the endogenous variable are similar, i.e. $\hat{Y}_a - \hat{Y}_b$ is small. Effectively this means classifying areas a and b according to the values of the exogenous variables $(C$ and $R)$. The logic is that regions should be defined for policy purposes according to the cause of their economic malaise, rather than its symptoms.

(iii) To classify a and b into the same region if the difference between the actual and estimated value of the endogenous variable is similar in both areas, i.e. if $(Y_a - \hat{Y}_a) - (Y_b - \hat{Y}_b)$ is small. Thus, if average incomes are higher in area a than its industrial structure and urbanisation would predict, but lower in area b than its industrial structure and urbanisation would predict, then a and b would not be classified into the same region. The unexplained variance (or 'regional factor' as it is sometimes called) is positive in the former case and negative in the latter. Note, however, that using 'region' to explain spatial variation merely signifies that the investigator has not finished his problem, since the regional factor only exists because some important exogenous variable (or variables) has been omitted. Thus, classifying regions in this way is the equivalent of classifying them according to the value of the omitted exogenous variable(s).

A slight variant of this approach is to classify a and b into the same region according to the parameters of the regression equation applied to time-series data.

Given $Y = A + \alpha C + \beta R$, then areas a and b would be classified into the same region only if $(\alpha_a - \alpha_b)$ and/or $(\beta_a - \beta_b)$ are small. This means that regional groupings are composed of areas in which average incomes respond similarly to changes in industrial structure and/or urbanisation. If the objective of equalising regional incomes is to be implemented through policies towards industrial structure and/or urbanisation, then regions will be internally homogeneous in their response.

The third problem, of introducing a contiguity constraint, is related to the number of regions selected. A contiguity constraint dictates that two areas cannot be regarded as being in the same region unless they are adjoining. This is normally introduced by geographers in defining regions, but is not strictly necessary for economic policy purposes. In the extreme case we would have a situation similar to that in the U.K. in the period 1960–6 when the areas in receipt of the benefits of regional policy were defined as those Local Employment Exchanges where a high rate of unemployment (taken by the Board of Trade as $4\frac{1}{2}$ per cent or more) existed, or was thought to be imminent. This policy did pose problems because of its fragmentary nature, and especially because areas were scheduled and de-scheduled according to short-term changes in their economic prosperity. Nevertheless it provides a clear example of regions being defined in terms of homogeneity without the introduction of a contiguity constraint. The main problems of omitting this constraint are the difficulty in generating economies in small development regions and the leakages from the income flows generated. *Ceteris paribus*, the smaller the region the smaller the multiplier effects of injections into the local economy. In larger groupings the propensity to import tends to be lower so that, for a given expenditure injection, the greater will be the final effect on regional income.

The polarisation concept provides a quite different approach to regional delineation and underlies much of the recent argument in favour of concentrating the incentives of regional policy in more narrowly defined growth centres. The two essential characteristics of polarised regions are that their constituent sub-areas are functionally interrelated and that they are arranged in a clear hierarchical order. Such regional groupings can be identified either by the use of theoretical models (usually of the gravity model type mentioned earlier) or by reference to empirical data on trade flows, workplace movements, freight traffic flows, telephone communications or other variables reflecting the intensity of intercommunication. Boudeville demonstrates some of these possibilities [38]. The important point is that, because of internal interconnection, economic developments within one part of the region will have effects throughout the rest of the region. Hence, the advocates of growth-centre policy argue, it is not necessary to provide blanket incentives for development over large areas: the instruments of policy should be concentrated on particular sub-areas within each of the less prosperous regions. This enables external economies to develop and, it is further argued, prevents regional policy leading to unwise location decisions in areas fundamentally not suited to industrial growth.

However, there are two important problems to consider. The first is that, while it is true that the effects of development will be transmitted throughout the 'internal hierarchy' of polarised regions, it is not certain whether these effects will be favourable or unfavourable. It is possible that spatial concentration of regional policy could lead to the intensification of economic problems in parts of the less prosperous regions. The situation is analogous to that of the 'grey areas' whose problems are accentuated by their proximity to Development Areas where financial inducements are offered to industrialists. Fundamentally, whether or not this is acceptable depends on the precise form in which the objectives of regional policy are specified. If a reduction of inter-regional variation in per capita incomes is sought, then a growth-centre policy appears favourable; if we are concerned with intra-regional equality, then it does not look so good. Secondly, like the homogeneity approach to regional delineation, the polarisation approach does not indicate the appropriate number of regions. Hence, the advocates of a growth-centre policy must adopt some other criterion to decide on the appropriate number of such centres. Clearly they face a dilemma between numerous centres, possibly too small to develop the full effects of external economies, and a few centres, each of which is potentially a new centre of congestion depending upon the (unknown) propulsive effects of the new development. The latter policy may also leave large areas in an even worse state than before as regards their ability to attract new developments themselves.

A compromise between these extremes can be derived from some suggestions by McCrone [55]. He distinguishes between the two grounds for spatial concentration of policy measures: increased efficiency of public expenditure and advantages of locational proximity between different industrial processes. There is little doubt that public expenditure, particularly on infrastructure, has a higher cost-effectiveness when concentrated in a few areas than when spread widely over a region and, as such, this provides a fairly clear argument for concentration. However, the advantages of locational proximity between different industrial processes may show much greater variation. The interrelationship in location of complementary firms was noted in Section 3 above, but the importance of such linkages varies between industries (see Isard, Schooler and Vietorisz [43]). The point is that the relevant geographical area for the establishment of industrial growth complexes is unlikely to be the same as that for achieving maximum efficiency in public expenditure. If, as McCrone suggests, it tends to be larger, the appropriate policy would seem to be that of concentrating public expenditure on growth centres while encouraging industry to make its own locational choice within more broadly defined development regions.

This sort of compromise approach is gaining favour in Western European policies, particularly in France, Belgium and the Netherlands. Norway relies almost exclusively on a growth-centre policy, partly because of its topological characteristics. At the other extreme, the U.K., Sweden and Italy concentrate on broad development area strategies and, to the extent that they offer a graduated system of regional incentives, provide the highest subsidies in the particular localities which have the most entrenched unemployment problems rather than the most potential for growth.

WORK TO THE WORKERS *v.* WORKERS TO THE WORK

Given that the regional problem is viewed as a spatial misallocation of the demand for and supply of labour and that

42

policy should be designed to secure greater harmony between the two distributions, there are two alternative strategies: to redirect the work to the workers or to redirect the workers to the work. Much of the discussion of regional policy, in the U.K. in particular, has been dominated by this disagreement over the relative advantages of policy to increase capital or labour mobility: see, for example, Richardson and West [33] and Needleman and Scott [32]. Let us briefly consider the arguments on each side, taking the 'workers to the work' school first.

The primary argument relates to the loss of economic growth which is caused by interference with the location of industry. It is contended that only when given free choice will businessmen select the optimal location for their plant; and that any restriction on that choice will lead either to the plant not being established at all, to it being established in an inferior location with resulting loss of efficiency, or to it being established in another country with no such restrictions. The result would be productivity losses and a rate of national economic growth below the attainable level. Reliance on labour mobility is said not to incur such economic costs because there is no interference with the location decisions of industry. Indeed, greater scope can be given in the firm's selection, because locations can be selected in the knowledge that even though current labour supplies may be inadequate, the regional policy towards labour migration will help to ensure that adequate supplies materialise. Richardson and West extend this argument further to suggest that labour mobility *per se* is a necessary condition for rapid national growth [33].

Most of the supplementary arguments for a policy of labour mobility are based upon the practical difficulties of devising a policy to influence capital mobility without encouraging inefficiency. For example, much of the subsidies paid to firms in the less prosperous areas is seen as encouraging industrial stagnation because no distinction is made between inefficient and efficient enterprises. Also it is possible that subsidies may be paid to firms expanding in the less prosperous areas who may have decided to expand there even without the subsidy. Hence, the cost to the public purse of regional policy is regarded as unnecessarily large in relation to the benefits secured.

The arguments advanced by the advocates of directing work to the workers usually begin by denying the above case. They suggest first of all that interference with private location decisions of firms does not necessarily reduce national economic growth. There are essentially three points here. The first is that, for many industries, costs vary little between alternative locations – see Nicholson [56] and Luttrell [54] – so that costs are increased little by steering firms away from their own selections. Secondly, firms do not necessarily select optimum sites when left to make their own location decisions; as we saw earlier, the choice is often determined by reference to satisficing rather than maximising criteria. Hence, redirection of industry need not necessarily involve additional private costs and could in some cases actually reduce them. The third point is that the whole basis of the 'loss of efficiency' argument is couched in terms of private rather than social costs. Since the very justification of intervention is couched in terms of this distinction, it seems strange to ignore it in considering the actual policies to be enacted!

This last point is itself supported by reference to three specific sources of divergence between private and social costs: congestion costs, social capital costs and cultural costs. The first of these, as we have already noted, are considered by firms only to the extent that they bear on the private costs. Hence, the argument that regional policy should avoid any direct influence on industrial location is highly dubious; it is tantamount to encouraging congestion, or at least to contending that the social costs of congestion are a price worth paying for the greater locational freedom given to industry.

The social capital argument has a similar theoretical basis. In making locational decisions, firms – and households, for that matter – do not fully consider the costs imposed on the community of providing social services in the chosen location. They need do so only to the extent that those costs are passed directly on to the consumers of the service and, since most social services are financed through general taxation, this direct charge is seldom levied. This provides an argument against allowing movement of labour out of areas where social capital (schools, hospitals, roads, etc.) is underutilised into areas where it is inadequate for existing demands. As an argument against encouraging workers to move to the work it is not conclusive, especially when the quality of social capital in the less prosperous regions is considered, but it does serve as another illustration that the social costs of encouraging capital mobility are usually less then those relating to labour mobility.

The cultural argument is fundamentally that migration of labour reduces inter-regional cultural variation. Emigrants tend to forget local dialects and shrug off their local customs, with the result that the greater the inter-regional labour movements the less diverse the country becomes from a cultural viewpoint. Many would consider this a social cost, and the fact that it cannot readily be quantified does not mean that it should be ignored.

Advocates of a 'work to the workers' policy also argue that the solution of the regional problem by labour migration is not only socially undesirable but economically inefficient. Firstly, it should be recognised that migration has a depressing effect on the economy of the donor region and an expansionary effect on the host region. There are three reasons for this: multiplier effects, investment effects and the effects on the quality of the work-force. When a migrant leaves a region the regional income is reduced by the value of his income (or welfare payments if he is unemployed) plus the multiplier effects induced by the corresponding reduction in consumption. Conversely, the income of the host region is increased by the value of his new personal income plus the multiplier effects induced by the resulting increase in consumption. To these effects can be added the probable impact of migration on regional investment. This is most clearly seen in terms of infrastructure expenditure: the host region will probably increase expenditure on social capital, causing further growth in income and the demand for labour in the region. On the other hand, income and demand for labour will fall further in the donor region because of the lower level of infrastructure expenditure needed to maintain social service standards. Thus, as Thirlwall emphasises, migration of labour may tend to exaggerate the regional problem by adding to the demand for labour in the regions already having excess demand and subtracting from the demand for labour in the regions already suffering from excess supply [34]. Finally, it should be recognised that labour migration has a long-run impact on the quality of the work-force. Friedmann notes that it is the

45

younger and more enterprising sectors of the population which tend to be most mobile [60]. Since such persons tend to become 'the entrepreneurs of tomorrow', the migration process will tend to add further to expansionary pressures in the already most prosperous regions at the expense of the least prosperous.

Lastly, there is the recurrent point about the nature of unemployment in the less prosperous regions. Some of those involuntarily out of work are not revealed in unemployment statistics, but are concealed in low activity rates. Many of these are married women who would not migrate to another area to obtain a job because it would involve the break-up of the family unit. Similar arguments may apply to teenagers staying on at school because of a shortage of opportunities locally. It should be clear that the effectiveness of labour mobility in removing regional unemployment differentials is curtailed by the joint nature of labour supply.

On balance, it seems that the arguments are weighted in favour of the 'work to the workers' school, and regional policy in the U.K. and elsewhere in Western Europe reflects this. Of course, it does not follow that the two policies are mutually exclusive and most governments recognise this by giving some assistance to labour mobility. Sweden and Finland have laid particular stress on measures to ease labour mobility and resulting social problems. The countries of the Common Market also rely quite heavily on mobility as an equilibrating mechanism both within and between nations. Mobility of both capital and labour is one of the basic tenets underlying the development of the EEC, but to date no common regional policy has been established and the six nations use a variety of policy measures designed to attract industry to their labour-surplus regions. In Canada the Area Development Agency and Atlantic Development Board offer incentives to firms setting up establishments in specified regions, while the Department of Forestry and Rural Development provides some assistance to labour leaving poor rural areas. Finally, the United Kingdom emphasises policies to divert industry, but among the existing policy instruments there are some which act on labour mobility. However, it should be noted that the policy of subsidising the costs of transferring key workers moving with their employers to a Development Area has its main influence on the mobility of capital. At first sight it would appear to be an encouragement to labour mobility, but the main effect is to increase the capital inflow into the less prosperous regions by reducing one of the problems associated with relocation of firms.

5 The Instruments of Regional Policy

EXPENDITURE POLICY

The first weapon of the government is to introduce a systematic regional variation in its expenditure on capital and/or current account. Such a policy is usually designed to secure a balance between aggregate demand and supply at the regional level. The result will be that the government runs a budget surplus in some regions and a budget deficit in others. This would normally occur even without an explicit regional dimension in the government's expenditure policy, so long as rates of taxation rise and rates of expenditure (on welfare payments, etc.) fall with increases in regional income. The explicit regional dimension in expenditure policy tends to increase these surpluses and deficits still more. The important question is their appropriate size, and this depends in turn on the policy objectives sought. Thus, given the goal of minimising regional unemployment differentials, deficits should be larger the greater the predicted level of unemployment and the smaller the value of the regional employment multiplier (which in turn is smaller the greater the region's marginal propensities to import and save).

Consider a second objective: regional income equalisation. Reiner has developed a simple model to show how a given expenditure (X) should be allocated between two regions $(a$ and $b)$ in order to equalise per capita incomes by a given target date [8]. Given the data on total incomes (Y) and population (N) in each region and the values of the regional multipliers (M), the value of government expenditure to be allocated to region a is determined as:

$$X_a = \frac{(Y_b + M_b X)/N_b - Y_a/N_a}{M_a/N_a + M_b/N_b}.$$

The value of expenditure to be allocated to region b is $X - X_a$. Such an allocation will equate per capita incomes in the two regions within the planning period (given certain assumptions about the offsetting nature of spillover effects between the regions and the constancy of multiplier value as between different sectors of expenditure injection).

Alternative criteria could be considered. One possibility is to allocate expenditure between regions in inverse proportion to per capita incomes. This gives a value for expenditure in region a of

$$X_a = \frac{(Y_b/N_b)X}{Y_b/N_b + Y_a/N_a}.$$

Such an allocation tends to produce a smaller share of expenditure for the less prosperous region than the allocation previously considered. This is because regional multiplier effects are ignored. Hence such an allocation will not result in complete equalisation (given regional multiplier values in excess of unity).

A still smaller share of central funds would be received by the poorer region if allocation were in direct proportion to population. Such a criterion underlies many expenditure policies, particularly those related to social services (although the allocation may be based on the distribution of some *subset* of the population, e.g. in allocating education expenditure according to numbers of school-age persons in the different regions). Whether an equalisation in prosperity results depends *inter alia* on the relative size of the regional multipliers: if the multiplier effect is greater in the least prosperous region, such an expenditure allocation will tend to narrow regional differences in economic prosperity, but if it is greater in the more prosperous region the tendency will be for regional differentials in prosperity to widen.

This demonstrates the importance of considering the leakages from regional economies in formulating regional plans. Regions are essentially open economies. Economic expansion in one region has spillover effects on other regions because of the import content of additional expenditure. This means that the geographical impact on incomes, employment, etc., of expenditure injections cannot be accurately forecast without knowledge of inter-regional and inter-sectoral relationships. Regional multipliers as used in Reiner's model can be estimated by methods such as those proposed by Archibald [36] and Steele [45]. However, such aggregated information still falls well short of the ideal. The multiplier effects of injections into the regional economy may vary considerably according to the sector where the injection takes place. Inter-regional input–output analysis can be of some help here. As noted earlier, it is essentially a static device but, given the sectoral distribution of the expenditure injection, it is possible to trace through the effects on final regional demand. Alternatively, given the desired impact on regional income, it is possible to use input–output analysis to determine how the size of the necessary injection varies according to sector.[1]

A related problem in considering the effect of different expenditure policies is that of long-run effects on the distribution of industry. Input–output analysis does not reflect these, but they are particularly relevant in the case of government infrastructure investment. This is often said to have an impact on the regional economy over and above its normal multiplier effect. Indeed, the common justification for using infrastructure improvements as an instrument of regional policy is that, by altering the relative attractiveness of regions to new developers, they change the spatial distribution of industry in the long run. There has been some systematic research of the determinants of industrial location – see, for example, the studies of Luttrell [54] and Cameron and Clark [49] – but this is inadequate for specifying the aggregate effect on infrastructure investment on long-term labour demand in different regions. Certainly, it is important to recognise that infrastructure investment may have propulsive effects. The emphasis on motorway development in Italy and Belgium and to a lesser extent in the United Kingdom is a reflection of this. However, as Brown argues in his note of dissent to the Hunt Report, the cost-effectiveness of infrastructure improvements would have to be shown to be greater than that of direct incentives to industry for it to be a preferred policy [57]. This is because the real cost – in terms of resources diverted from other uses – is

---

[1] A useful introduction to input–output analysis (including a chapter on regional applications) is C. Yan, *Introduction to Input–Output Economics* (Holt, Rinehart & Winston, New York, 1969).

relatively high. This would suggest that the best attitude to infrastructure investment is what the French call *accompagnement* rather than *entraînement* – accompanying population and industrial growth rather than attempting to induce it. However, this point cannot be strongly argued: we simply do not know enough about the strength of the complementarities between private and public investment. Moreover, if we believe that the government has a responsibility for planning regional development, and not just for correcting bottlenecks arising from private development, it follows that the government has an obligation to take the initiative in the development process.

This brings us to the general problem of using expenditure policies in regional development – that of opportunity costs. To direct a more than proportionate share of central funds to one region requires that expenditure be curtailed in others. Since much government expenditure is directly related to pressing social demands (for schools, roads, hospitals, etc.) the opportunity costs of this sort of reallocation are likely to become a strong political issue. This is especially true because the pressure on existing social capital is likely to be stronger in those areas which, according to policies of this sort, should have their share of government expenditure reduced.

However, there are various methods by which more direct government expenditure might be more widely used in the promotion of regional development. First, any government has relatively strong control over nationalised industries; and long-run changes could be implemented in their location, subject to the constraints imposed by the nature of the goods and services produced. Italy has used this policy in securing a higher share of industrial developments for the Mezzogiorno, but it has not been used widely elsewhere. Decentralisation of government offices is a second and related policy, and some progress has been made here in the U.K. where departments have established major administrative units in Scotland, Wales, Merseyside and the Northern Region. A further possibility is suggested by the siting of New Towns and industrial estates. These developments can be used not merely as remedies for intra-regional congestion but, given that the New Towns are planned as 'counter-magnets' rather than dormitory settlements, as a means of influencing the allocation of resources between regions. The creation of entirely new capital cities such as Canberra (Australia) and Brasilia (Brazil) are striking examples, although not entirely motivated by regional economic considerations. Finally, there is the public sector's position as a purchaser. The U.K. operates two schemes: contracts preference and general preference. Under the former, firms in the Development Areas are given an opportunity to obtain 25 per cent of an order if the lowest tender is from a firm outside the Development Areas, provided that there is no increase in the overall cost to the government. Under the latter, contracts are given automatically to firms in the Development Areas if their tenders are equal in all respects to those received from firms outside the Development Areas. Such schemes are obviously very moderate, but could be extended by giving more positive preferences to the less prosperous regions, even at a cost in terms of higher prices for supplies. As emphasised in a recent Labour Party publication, the effects of such a policy could be revolutionary [51].

PRICE POLICY

Price policies are defined as any regionally discriminatory subsidies and taxes. These may apply either to inputs or outputs of the productive process: the point is that they change the relative prices between regions.

Changes in input prices

The most obvious examples of such a policy are investment grants, payroll taxes and subsidies (or rebates such as the U.K. Regional Employment Premium) and low-interest loans. The desired effect is a reduction in costs of production in the less prosperous regions relative to those in the more prosperous regions, leading to a relative expansion of production in the former areas. Such policies have been widely used in France, the Netherlands, Sweden and West Germany as well as in the U.K. There are two recurrent problems: whether to concentrate on changing the price of labour or capital, and whether more selectivity should be applied in the distribution of such sub-sidies, grants and so on.

The capital *v.* labour subsidy argument has received fairly extensive treatment in the economic literature. Borts, for example, demonstrates that a wage subsidy is always preferable to a capital subsidy, but his model is based on the assumption that the supply of labour is perfectly inelastic while the supply of capital is perfectly elastic [29]. Different assumptions yield opposite conclusions. It is important not to fall into the trap of forgetting that regionally differentiated subsidies have two effects: (1) on the demand for factor inputs by firms already established in the favoured regions, and (2) on the long-run distribution of industry as between regions.

The first can be analysed in terms of the usual comparative static methodology. Consider the effects of a capital subsidy on the level of employment. There are essentially two possibilities as shown in Figs. 2 and 3.

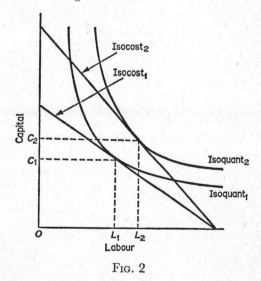

Fig. 2

In each case the effect of a capital subsidy is to change the relative factor prices from isocost$_1$ to isocost$_2$. In Fig. 2 this leads to an increase in capital utilised (from OC_1 to OC_2) but also an increase in labour employed (from OL_1 to OL_2): this is because the output effect on the demand for labour of the relative price change outweighs the factor substitution effect.

53

In Fig. 3 the effect of the subsidy is to increase capital employed (from OC_1 to OC_2) but to *reduce* labour employed (from OL_1 to OL_2): here the output effect on the demand for labour is outweighed by the substitution effect. It follows that whether or not capital subsidies lead to increased employment depends on the nature of production functions. This condition does not apply to labour subsidies: these always

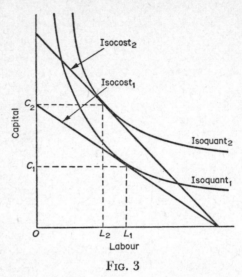

FIG. 3

tend to increase employment because the output and substitution effects on the demand for labour act in the same direction. A subsidy on labour will lead to substitution of labour for capital (depending on the elasticity of technical substitution) *and* to an increase in demand for labour resulting from the tendency of subsidies to lead to expansion of output. It follows that, given an objective of reducing regional differences in the unemployment of labour, a policy of regionally differentiated taxes and subsidies on labour will have a more certain effect than one based on capital taxes and subsidies. This is a useful general rule, but subject to three reservations. Firstly, there is the question of the percentage of labour costs in total costs of production: if this is small, so too will be the effect on employment creation of labour subsidies. Secondly, there is the possibility that capital subsidies might have a more direct effect on the level of labour productivity, leading to increases in regional income and the possibility of demand-led growth (as opposed to the export-led growth which follows from regional price reductions). Thirdly, there is the whole question of business objectives: businessmen may be either more or less influenced by different subsidies than their actual post-tax value would suggest. In this case no analysis of the relative merits of capital and labour subsidies which assumes profit maximisation is strictly relevant.

Turning to the effects on the long-term distribution of labour, we can only say that the relative effectiveness of capital and labour subsidies depends on their relative attractiveness to potentially mobile firms. Assuming profit maximisation, labour subsidies would have a greater attraction to labour-intensive firms, and this is presumably the desired effect, given that the regional problem is viewed in terms of unemployment. Otherwise, economic theory as such has relatively little to say on this subject: it becomes a purely empirical question of whether more employment opportunities are generated by incoming firms as a result of an x per cent capital subsidy or an x per cent labour subsidy.

Recent policy changes have tended to favour the use of labour subsidies in reducing regional unemployment differentials. The introduction of the Regional Employment Premium in the U.K. in 1966 can be regarded as a step in this direction, but even now, as a percentage of average wage costs, this is less than the capital subsidies offered. It is not surprising that some of the new industry attracted to the Development Areas is highly capital-intensive. Such industries may provide a basis for long-term growth in the regions, but their short-term direct impact on employment is often very small (excluding the additional employment generated by the construction process itself). Other European countries have had a similar experience, but the capital v. labour subsidy argument has tended to become obscured by the discussion of the relative merits of growth-centre and broad development region strategies. Because the criterion for the selection of growth areas relates more to their potential for development than to their current economic hardship, attention is switched away from the reduction of existing regional unemployment differentials as the *raison d'être* for regional policy. Policy becomes defined in terms of more vaguely defined long-run objectives relating to inter-regional balance. This reduction in emphasis on short-run labour market problems thereby reduces the apparent weight of the case for relating subsidies to numbers unemployed. It only reduces their *real* weight if policy objectives are explicitly defined in terms of some other objective than the reduction in current unemployment.

The question of selectivity is a different one from both the theoretical and practical viewpoints. Most of the inducements to expand in the Development Areas of the U.K. are automatic (with the principal exception of building grants which are conditional upon employment creation), unlike in France and Italy where they are normally restricted to approved projects. The oft-repeated argument for the latter sort of policy is that without selectivity much of the grants and subsidies paid are wasted because, instead of increasing employment, they go mainly to increase profits. This is usually considered objectionable, particularly where the effect is to keep inefficient firms in business. However, the argument is inconclusive. Increased profits may lead to employment expansion elsewhere in the regional economy, depending on saving and import propensities. More fundamentally, it is the social benefits of keeping employment levels up in the regions which provides one of the arguments underlying the case for regional price policy. Thus, from the wider social viewpoint, the support of firms which are inefficient in terms of private economies is not necessarily inefficient. In any case, it is extremely difficult to devise a system which achieves selectivity without doing considerable violence to criteria of efficiency and equity. Selectivity requires that bodies be established to decide rates of grants, tax, etc., on the basis of number of jobs created, particular job skills involved, particular location chosen, and so on. Bureaucratic decision-making of considerable skill is required if recurrent conflict between government and industry is to be avoided. The separate scrutiny of each firm's expansion proposals must lead to delays in development and invite accusations of arbitrariness and corruption.

Changes in output prices
A regionally differentiated system of export rebates, taxes and subsidies could be established in order to change output prices on a regional basis. Such a policy is not directly sub-

stitutable for one bearing on input prices, but its objectives are similar in that the intention is to steer growth to the less prosperous regions. It could be considered to operate like a regional devaluation. The central problem is that, like any output tax or subsidy, its effect depends on demand and supply elasticities. There will be relatively little direct impact on output levels when price elasticities are low. Even when demand and supply elasticities are high, there will be little employment creation in circumstances where capital/output ratios are high at the margin. Clearly, both market and production conditions must be right for output price policies to have the desired regional effect. This uncertainty, together with the problems of implementing output subsidy policies in times when deflationary policies are being operated nationally, accounts for the general reluctance of governments to use such a policy.

A regionally discriminatory tax on profits is an alternative measure, albeit not directly designed to change output prices. It would have no direct effect on output and employment of firms already located in the less prosperous areas (assuming profit maximisation). However, it would affect the relative attractiveness of different areas for firms considering expansion or relocation. The problem is that, like any cut in the rate of tax on profits, the saving is greater for the firm with high profitability than for the one with low profitability. This may be justified in terms of its incentive effects, but poses some problems for firms in the less prosperous areas. For example, it means that the tax concessions are of least value to firms in the early years of establishment when they are facing high initial costs and require the assistance most. Such considerations underlay the 1967 policy change in Canada, when incentives to locate in the least prosperous areas were switched from the form of tax incentives to that of cash grants (see Brewis [59]).

CONTROLS

Controls can be considered as an extreme case of price policy: either permission for development is granted (implying zero tax) or it is refused (implying an infinite tax). Such is the case with Industrial Development Certificates and Office Development Permits in the U.K. IDCs were introduced in 1947 and all new development proposals over a certain size require such permission, although it is seldom refused in the Development Areas. Control of office development was added in 1964 in an attempt to control congestion in the South-east and, later, in the Midlands. Together these instruments constitute a more rigorous control than is found in any other country of Western Europe. The French do attempt to restrict development in the Paris region, but the redistribution effects are much more localised.

The first point to note is that the existence of controls alongside of other regional policies (such as investment grants and employment subsidies) is an admission of the inadequacy of these latter policies. If they were successful, no controls would be needed. However, of the two possible reasons for failure of regional price policies, only one provides a good justification for controls. The two possibilities are that the level of grants, taxes, subsidies, etc., is not that required for reconciliation of private and social costs in alternative locations, and that firms do not react to the grants, taxes, subsidies, etc., in a way which brings about an optimum resource allocation. The former requires an increase in the expenditure on locational inducements; the latter may justify the use of controls. For instance, if businessmen do not seek maximum-profit locations, then their choice of site may be quite unresponsive to regional input and output price differentials. (It may be more sensitive to the availability of golf courses or to the dictates of their wives!) Hence, even with 'ideal' regional price policies which equate private and social costs in all locations, bureaucratic censure may be called for in the interests of the less prosperous regions.[1]

One problem with controls is to estimate their impact on aggregate industrial expansion. Actually, there is very little evidence, either of the effect on the growth of total output or

[1] This is just one special case of 'second-best' economic policies. Failure of firms to maximise profits means that one of the usual assumptions of economic theory is violated; if it cannot be re-established, then the ideal policy may differ from that suggested by the usual analysis of allocative efficiency. These 'second-best' problems are as thorny in regional economic policy as in any other aspect of economics.

on levels of productivity. The Confederation of British Industry have made studies, but their conclusion that IDC control should be scrapped, both because it 'is applied more liberally than is widely recognised' and because 'growth is being lost . . . on account of the strict application of IDC control' [50] is clearly inconsistent. What is certain is that any relaxation of development controls in countries like Britain and France would lead to increased congestion at the centre and a smaller share of industrial growth in the less prosperous regions. This suggests that, rather than abolish controls, consideration should be given to replacing them by a system of congestion taxes. These could be regarded as part of the scheme outlined earlier for a gradation of regions from those in which development is taxed to those in which it is highly subsidised. Such a system has the added advantage that the tax paid by industrialists expanding in congested zones could meet at least some of the social costs imposed on the community. Moreover, the introduction of a congestion tax would serve to emphasise the important point that reductions in national economic growth are not necessarily inconsistent with maximum social welfare. Thus, in addition to reallocative effects, a congestion tax might have an effect on aggregate output but, given that the congestion tax is designed to reconcile private and social costs, this effect can be seen as a move towards rather than away from the optimum level of economic activity.

REDUCING FACTOR IMMOBILITY

As noted earlier, the reduction of factor immobility is the most obvious implication for policy stemming from resource reallocation theories of regional growth. There are three main ways in which policy can act on factor immobility: by removal of market imperfections causing immobility, by long-run policies to change the qualities of the factors themselves least consistent with mobility, and by direct subsidies to migrant factors.

In the first category would fall policies to increase labour mobility through encouragement of local rather than national wage-bargaining systems. The latter procedure prevents regional income differentials fully reflecting regional unemployment differentials. Hence, the incentives to migration will be inadequate to ensure that the regional unemployment differentials are reduced. A system of local wage bargaining would permit the market mechanisms to work more freely. A similar effect would result from abolition of minimum-wage legislation (where it exists). This is another barrier to the free operation of the price system in the labour market, and hence reduces migratory flows. Alternatively the government could intervene by actually levying additional taxes on the incomes of labour in the prosperous regions and by reducing taxes on earned income in the less prosperous regions. There would be considerable administrative difficulties, but the general effect should be to make post-tax wages approximate more closely to equilibrium levels in the different regions. Note, however, that all these policies will conflict with equity objectives in the short run; this accounts for their political unpopularity.

Inadequate information constitutes another major market imperfection. As noted earlier, most location theories assume perfect knowledge. In fact, both labour and capital are inefficiently immobile because of lack of awareness of opportunities in other regions. The role of the government is clear in this respect: to publicise nationally opportunities for investment in regions where labour is the abundant factor and opportunities for employment in regions where capital is abundant. Such information spread may also have value in terms of the transmission of technical progress. The least prosperous regions frequently have capital stock of older average age than in the more prosperous regions. The spread of new techniques to such areas will improve their long-run competitive position.

The second group of policies towards mobility relate to the quality of the factors themselves. Subsidies for education and retraining come in this category because, by increasing the range of jobs a man can undertake, one normally increases the possibility of his finding employment in another region (or, indeed, in his own region). Thus, in the U.K. generous grants have been given both for 'on the job' training as well as retraining in government centres. Such policies help in reducing the problem of unemployment resulting from overdependence of particular areas on particular industries. There may also be long-term effects on attitudes to migration, but it is not possible to estimate this without more extensive attitude surveys.

The third main method of encouraging migration is by direct subsidy. This differs from what we earlier called price policy in that instead of giving blanket incentives to development in the less prosperous regions through changing relative prices of inputs and/or outputs on a geographical basis, incentives are provided only to incoming factors. This could be applied to labour through removal subsidies or grants, temporary housing subsidies or other means to defray resettlement costs. It could also be applied to capital, but the problem with such a policy is that it gives no comparable incentives to firms already in the less prosperous regions to expand their outputs. Hence, a concerted effort to expand the demand for labour in the less prosperous regions through capital migration subsidies would require that such a policy be supplemented by some form of encouragement to locally established firms.

Finally, it should be emphasised that mobility of labour may be a socially undesirable method of solving the regional problem, even if it is an economically efficient one. Factor demand and supply distributions are spatially interdependent: we noted earlier that labour mobility can add to inflationary pressures in the prosperous regions and cause further unemployment in the less prosperous regions. Moreover, labour migration can have social costs in terms of family unity or preservation of regional cultures. Perhaps the most balanced policy towards factor mobility is that of removing barriers through the provision of information, education, etc. To go further than this is less easily justifiable. The irony is that those right-wingers who advocate the solution of regional problems through increased inter-regional mobility are frequently the staunchest defenders of barriers to mobility at the international level!

6 Remaining Issues

Regional policy instruments of the sort suggested in the last section have been widely applied. However, it is very difficult to evaluate their success. Regional policy has had a relatively short history in most countries and seldom have the objectives been precisely quantified. Hence, the evaluation of success is not possible in any quantitative manner. Moreover, of course, such evaluation requires knowledge of what would have happened to regional variations in average income, unemployment, and so on, in the absence of policy. Thus, a fully-fledged model of regional development, including policy variables, is required. Dynamic as well as static influences should be incorporated, since part of the impact of regional policies will normally be in changing structural characteristics and the pattern of inter-regional/inter-sectoral linkages. At present we have no such operational model.

However, even in the absence of such a systematic evaluation, it is clear that policies have not realised expectations. Regional inequalities persist in all countries. In the U.K., for example, relative unemployment differentials between regions are very similar to what they were thirty-five years ago, despite the array of regional policy measures used during the period. The regional variation in per capita incomes has also been remarkably stable in the post-war period. It seems likely that inequality would have tended to increase if there had been no regional policies in operation. Certainly some countries, such as Japan, Yugoslavia and India, have actually suffered from widening regional income differentials in the post-war years. The evidence is generally consistent with Williamson's thesis that inequalities tend to widen, then narrow as a country passes through the various stages of economic development [64]. The problem is that the stages of economic development and policies enacted are not independent; it is in the developed countries that regional policies are most strenuously pursued. Hence, part of the tendency towards increased equality in countries like Canada, Sweden, West Germany and the Netherlands may be attributed to the effects of policy. This makes it all the more worrying for countries like Italy, France and the U.K. which have largely failed to reduce regional inequalities despite expensive policy measures.

Such considerations make it more appropriate to end with a section on 'remaining issues' than with one on 'conclusions'.

First, there is the question of the appropriate level of expenditure from central funds on regional policy measures. There are two problems: measuring the net cost of policy measures and measuring the opportunity cost of that expenditure. As Needleman and Scott emphasise, much of the expenditure of regional policy is not a net cost in that there is a return to central funds [32]. The extra incomes generated in the less prosperous regions by capital and labour subsidies, grants, etc., yield additional revenue from taxation. Also the reduced unemployment leads to a saving of welfare expenditures. Estimating the value of such feedbacks is a very difficult problem, albeit relatively easy compared with the other necessary step: the estimation of the opportunity cost. This, of course, requires some estimation of the returns at the margin of other forms of government expenditure, in housing, education, overseas aid, agricultural subsidies, 'defence' and so on. Only then is one really in a position to argue for an increased or a reduced expenditure on regional policy. The ideal allocation of expenditure between competing ends is that where opportunity costs are equal. Conceptually this is unexceptionable: the problem is one of evaluation. The variables involved are so fundamentally linked with social and political considerations that no economist has ever attempted the full cost-benefit statement. The decision on allocating central funds must necessarily be a political one. Given this situation, the advocates of a stronger regional policy would be well advised to emphasise the potential contribution of regional policy to the achievement of national economic objectives (e.g. a lower rate of inflation for a given level of unemployment) and to the achievement of national political objectives (e.g. the maintenance of internal political unity).

A second major problem is the choice of weapons. We have

briefly considered the arguments for the various policy instruments, but in many circumstances they would appear to be relatively close substitutes. Countries with similar regional problems have adopted a variety of instruments (ranging from infrastructure improvements, controls on factory and office development, measures to increase capital mobility and measures to ease the problems associated with labour mobility, to the siting of new towns) and in part it is this experimental variety which makes it difficult to assess the impact of the individual measures. What is worth emphasising, however, is the importance of individual preference functions and, in particular, the evidence on the incidence of non-maximising locational objectives. Given that location decisions are taken by satisficers rather than maximisers, the simplicity and conspicuousness of regional policy instruments may be more important than their actual monetary value.

Thirdly, there is the problem of the link between regional economic planning and physical (or land-use) planning. One obviously has repercussions on the other, but there is seldom simultaneous consideration because of the separate institutions involved. Land-use planning is usually undertaken at a local level, while economic planning is the responsibility of the central government. Indeed, it is now being realised in countries like Sweden, Norway and Finland that the local government units are frequently too small even for the function of land-use planning, let alone regional economic planning. Amalgamation into larger units is proceeding, albeit not without local protests. France is at the other extreme, and suffers from problems of over-centralisation in decision-making. Policies tend to be formulated by central authorities which do not arouse local initiative and enterprise. French attempts to surmount this problem have been disappointing so far, judged both by the patchiness of the results of policy on the prosperity of the south and west and by the continuing problems of political unity. Similarly in the U.K., attempts to integrate local and broader regional planning have met with limited success. Much hope has been centred on the eight Regional Planning Councils set up in 1964–5. The responsibilities and achievements of these bodies are well summarised by McCrone [55], but it is clear that the experiment has been of dubious success. Each Council has produced reports on recommended developments, but these are unco-ordinated and are conspicuously lacking in cost calculations. The Councils' links upwards to the central government and downwards to local authorities are both weak. Thus, the problem of linking economic and physical planning can be seen as one particular aspect of the problem of decentralised decision-making. The goal must be to find an administrative structure which permits decentralisation without sacrifice in terms of co-ordination. This is an ideal to which we should try to approximate.

The final issue is the impact of integration on regional problems. The formation of blocs such as the EEC both changes the spatial distribution of economic activities and restricts the ability of each member country to deal with the problems within its own boundaries. The interesting report of the OECD shows how most countries within Western Europe have their own centre–periphery problems while, looking at the area as a whole, there is an overall centre–periphery problem [62]. Indeed, the broader the area taken, the greater the differentials in economic prosperity; what may be regarded as a poor region within one nation may be rich relative to other nations. In this way the regional problem converges with the problem of the less developed countries of the world. If we are willing to apply the arguments of inter-regional equity and efficiency on a world-wide rather than a national level, then policies to assist the less developed countries must have the highest priority. To take this broader view of regional problems provides a valuable perspective, one which is made the more important by the loss of perspective implicit in recent tendencies towards isolationist policies.

Select Bibliography

POLICY OBJECTIVES

[1] W. Isard and T. Reiner, 'Regional and National Economic Planning', in *Regional Economic Planning*, ed. W. Isard and J. H. Cumberland (OEEC, Paris, 1961) pp. 19–38. This introductory paper argues the case for consistency in the formulation of regional and national policies, as well as suggesting some applications of input–output and industrial complex analysis. Other papers in the same volume provide case studies of regional planning in Greece, Italy, Spain, Turkey, Yugoslavia and Puerto Rico.

[2] C. L. Leven, 'Establishing Goals for Regional Economic Development', *Journal of the American Institute of Planners* (May 1964) pp. 100–10; reprinted in J. Friedmann and W. Alonso, *Regional Development and Planning: A Reader* (M.I.T. Press, Cambridge, Mass., 1964) pp. 581–98. Leven stresses the need to specify explicit goals in the formulation of regional development programmes and demonstrates how a linear programming model can handle alternative policy objectives.

[3] M. C. McGuire and H. A. Garn, 'The Integration of Equity and Efficiency Criteria in Public Project Selection', *Economic Journal* (Dec 1969) pp. 882–93. The authors show how the trade-off between efficiency and equity criteria can be identified. Past decisions on allocation of central funds between regionally specific projects are analysed and the empirical results reveal interesting inconsistencies on the part of the decision-makers.

[4] K. Mera, 'Tradeoff between Aggregate Efficiency and Interregional Equity: A Static Analysis', *Quarterly Journal of Economics* (1967) pp. 658–74. Unlike the study by

McGuire and Garn [3], this work is purely theoretical. The apparatus of Edgeworth boxes provides the framework for demonstrating how the cost of pursuing policies for inter-regional equity can be measured in terms of the sacrifice in aggregate efficiency.

[5] E. Nevin, 'The Case for Regional Policy', *Three Banks Review* (Dec 1966) pp. 30–46. A useful introductory essay, stressing the economic, technological and social factors underlying the increasing concern with regionalism.

[6] H. S. Perloff, 'Problems of Assessing Regional Economic Progress', in *Regional Income: Studies in Income and Wealth*, vol. 21 (National Bureau of Economic Research, Princeton U.P., 1957) pp. 35–62. Perloff lists various indices of regional prosperity and discusses some problems encountered in their measurement. The problem of regional delineation is also emphasised; in particular, that ideal boundaries change both over time and according to the problem being investigated. Other papers in the same volume also deal with the interrelationship between the problems of defining regions and of estimating regional incomes.

[7] T. Reiner, 'Organising Regional Investment Criteria', *Regional Science Association: Papers and Proceedings* (1963) pp. 63–72. This article is complementary to that listed as [8] but is worth consulting because of its simple exposition of the linear programming method of resolving conflicting objectives. Also the importance of regional delineation is stressed: the classification of regional groupings influences the difficulty of achieving specified goals.

[8] T. Reiner, 'Sub-national and National Planning: Decision Criteria', *Regional Science Association: Papers and Proceedings* (1965) pp. 107–36. Reiner shows how the allocation of central funds between regions can be determined by reference to the regional objectives. Also, he demonstrates how the opportunity cost of alternative allocations depends on the size of aggregate regional multipliers. However, his simple models do not explicitly consider the possibility of disaggregation by sector leading to different multiplier values.

CONTRIBUTIONS FROM REGIONAL ECONOMICS

Some of the best articles on regional economics have been collected together in the following books:

[9] R. D. Dean, W. H. Leahy and D. L. McKee, *Spatial Economic Theory* (Free Press, New York, 1970). This includes classic articles on location theory. In addition to the usual partial equilibrium approach there is emphasis on providing a synthesis via general equilibrium analysis.

[10] J. Friedmann and W. Alonso, *Regional Development and Planning: A Reader* (M.I.T. Press, Cambridge, Mass., 1964). This excellent volume contains thirty-five articles, ranging from location theory to regional development theory and the formulation of regional policy.

[11] L. Needleman, *Regional Analysis: Selected Readings* (Penguin Books, Harmondsworth, 1968). Another useful collection containing, *inter alia*, Meyer's general survey of regional economics, Chenery's policy model for development of southern Italy and Williamson's empirical study of regional inequalities.

[12] H. Perloff and L. Wingo, *Issues in Urban Economics*, published for Resources for the Future Inc. (Johns Hopkins Press, Baltimore, 1968). These selections refer to urban rather than regional policy issues. In addition to sections on city growth and intra-metropolitan development there is a useful section on the public sector. The articles by Margolis and Hirsch on the demand for and supply of public services are particularly useful.

The following books and articles also contain matter which is either directly relevant to the formulation of regional economic policy or indirectly through increasing our understanding of the process of regional growth.

[13] W. Alonso, *Location and Land Use: Towards a General Theory of Land Rent* (Harvard U.P., Cambridge, Mass., 1964). After considering partial equilibrium models of the household, firm and farm, Alonso presents an analysis of market equilibrium. Emphasis is placed on the bid

price curves of the various economic agents, providing insights into how the demand for accessibility influences intra-urban land-use patterns.

[14] M. Beckman, *Location Theory* (Random House, New York, 1968). Beckman restricts his scope to spatial micro-economics and, by using what he calls a 'geometric-intuitive' approach, attempts to develop a general theory of the allocation of economic activities in space. However, the results are somewhat piecemeal although the partial analyses of industrial location and land use are valuable.

[15] M. L. Greenhut, *A Theory of the Firm in Economic Space* (Appleton-Century-Crofts, New York, 1970). This is a valuable fusion of location theory with micro-economic analysis, extending some of the author's earlier work on the profit-maximising location.

[16] H. Hotelling, 'Stability in Competition', *Economic Journal* (Mar 1929) pp. 41–57; reprinted in R. D. Dean, W. H. Leahy and D. L. McKee, *Spatial Economic Theory* (Free Press, New York, 1970), and in American Economic Association, *Readings in Price Theory* (Allen & Unwin, London, 1953). A pioneer article, showing the inter-relationships between price competition and location in the duopoly situation.

[17] W. Isard, *Location and the Space Economy* (M.I.T. Press, Cambridge, Mass., 1956). A standard reference on location theory. Isard lays emphasis on the role of transport inputs, but does go on to synthesise both cost and revenue considerations in a general theory of location.

[18] E. J. Mishan, *The Costs of Economic Growth* (Staples Press, London, 1967). This book is not centrally concerned with regional policy, although it does contain a section dealing with urban problems. Its value is in showing, *inter alia*, how the failure to deal with externalities leads to non-optimal situations. The style ranges entertainingly between formal statements of welfare economics and personal reflections on social and economic trends.

[19] G. Myrdal, *Economic Theory and Underdeveloped Regions* (Methuen, London, 1957). This is a simple exposition of the role of circular and cumulative causation in perpetuating regional inequalities. Myrdal has relatively

little to say on policies to counter this process because he views the role of the state as an integral part of it. For a less pessimistic view with specific proposals for countering centre–periphery problems, see Friedmann [60].

[20] G. M. Neutze, *Economic Policy and the Size of Cities* (Australian National U.P., Canberra, 1965). The best empirical study of congestion costs. Conclusions are tentative but confirm the concept of an optimum urban size somewhere in the population range between 200,000 and one million.

[21] D. C. North, 'Location Theory and Regional Economic Growth', *Journal of Political Economy* (June 1955) pp. 243–58; reprinted in J. Friedmann and W. Alonso, *Regional Development and Planning: A Reader* (M.I.T. Press, Cambridge, Mass., 1964). North applies the concept of the economic base at the regional level in an attempt to explain the crucial role of exports in regional growth. He suggests that this provides a better explanation of U.S. experience than do models which concentrate on the stages of regional development.

[22] H. O. Nourse, *Regional Economics* (McGraw-Hill, New York and London, 1968). An introductory text. Nourse assumes little knowledge of economics and explains the general analytical techniques fully before he deals with specific regional applications. The result is that he does not cover much ground compared, say, with Richardson's text [23].

[23] H. W. Richardson, *Regional Economics* (Weidenfeld & Nicolson, London, 1969). This is an excellent survey of regional economic theory. It deals with location theory, urban structure, regional income and growth, and ends with two useful chapters on policy.

[24] H. Siebert, *Regional Economic Growth: Theory and Policy* (International Textbook Company, London, 1969). An ambitious attempt to formulate a general theory of regional growth. The two chapters on policy issues are not well integrated with the rest of the book, but are worth consulting because of the discussion of interrelated goals and decision criteria for regional policies.

[25] A. Smithies, 'Optimum Location in Spatial Competition', *Journal of Political Economy* (June 1941) pp. 423–39;

reprinted in R. D. Dean, W. H. Leahy and D. L. McKee, *Spatial Economic Theory* (Free Press, New York, 1970) and in American Economic Association, *Readings in Price Theory* (Allen & Unwin, London, 1953). A reformulation of the analysis of Hotelling [16]. Relaxing the assumption of inelastic demand reduces the tendency for competitors to cluster together at the centre of the market. Further, it is demonstrated how the equilibrium location pattern depends on freight rates, but these are only considered in respect of the transport of outputs: the cost of transporting inputs is ignored.

[26] C. M. Tiebout, 'Exports and Regional Economic Growth', *Journal of Political Economy* (Apr 1956) pp. 160–9; reprinted in J. Friedmann and W. Alonso, *Regional Development and Planning: A Reader* (M.I.T. Press, Cambridge, Mass., 1964). This is a reply to North [21]. Tiebout says that the export base theory can be fitted within a more general theory of income determination, and that not to do so places too much emphasis on exports to the neglect of other growth stimuli.

STRATEGIES FOR POLICY

[27] G. C. Archibald, 'The Phillips Curve and the Distribution of Unemployment', *Papers and Proceedings of the American Economic Association* (May 1969). Using regression techniques, Archibald finds that the addition of a regional dispersion variable increases the ability to explain rates of inflation in terms of unemployment. It follows that policies to reduce regional unemployment differentials can help to shift the national Phillips curve leftwards.

[28] P. A. Bird and A. P. Thirlwall, 'The Incentive to Invest in the New Development Areas', *District Bank Review* (June 1967) pp. 24–45. This is primarily a discussion of the post-tax value of regional policy incentives introduced in the U.K. in 1966. The authors conclude that the new inducements to firms to move to the less prosperous regions are likely to be little more effective than those previously offered, and recommend that more attention be given to infrastructure improvements.

71

[29] G. H. Borts, 'Criteria for Evaluation of Regional Development Programmes', in W. Z. Hirsch, *Regional Accounts for Policy Decisions* (Johns Hopkins Press, Baltimore, 1966). Borts argues the case for choosing between policies according to the social rate of return on investment. This is defined – regrettably without discussion of alternatives – in terms of national product. It is then demonstrated that such a criterion favours labour rather than capital subsidies in regional policies, but this only follows if the supply of capital is considered perfectly elastic and the supply of labour perfectly inelastic.

[30] C. Clark, 'Industrial Location and Economic Potential', *Lloyds Bank Review* (Oct 1966) pp. 1–17. The concept of economic potential has a long history in regional analysis. In applying it to the U.K., Clark argues the case for a system of regionally differentiated payroll taxes and subsidies. The proposals of the Labour Party study group [51] derive from this.

[31] C. P. Harris and A. P. Thirlwall, 'Inter-regional Variations in Cyclical Sensitivity to Unemployment in the U.K. 1949–64', *Bulletin of the Oxford Institute of Economics and Statistics* (1968) pp. 55–66. The authors apply standardisation techniques in an attempt to distinguish between inter-industry and intra-industry causes of differences in regional instability. The latter effects are shown to dominate, suggesting that 'industrial structure' is a relatively poor explanation of the amplitude of regional cycles.

[32] L. Needleman and B. Scott, 'Regional Problems and the Policy of Attracting Industry to the Peripheral Regions of Britain', in *The Lothians Regional Survey and Plan* (H.M.S.O., Edinburgh, 1966). This, and the similar articles by Needleman in *Urban Studies* (Nov 1964) and *Lloyds Bank Review* (Jan 1965), provide strong support for the policy of taking workers to the work. Crude calculations are also made to show that the scale of expenditure on policy instruments is uneconomically low.

[33] H. W. Richardson and E. G. West, 'Must We Always Take Work to the Workers?', *Lloyds Bank Review* (Jan 1964) pp. 35–48. An opposing view to Needleman and

Scott [32], this argues the case for more emphasis on labour mobility. The authors contend that this is a more effective way of reducing unemployment, at least in conditions where the overall unemployment level is relatively low.

[34] A. P. Thirlwall, 'Migration and Regional Unemployment', *Westminster Bank Review* (Nov 1966) pp. 31–44. Another contribution to the capital *v.* labour mobility controversy. Thirlwall concentrates on the interaction between labour demand and supply distributions. He demonstrates how inter-regional labour migration may have expansionary effects on the currently most prosperous regions and concludes that the reduction of regional uncmployment differentials may require policies actually to restrict labour movements.

[35] A. P. Thirlwall, 'Regional Phillips Curves', *Bulletin of the Oxford Institute of Economics and Statistics* (Feb 1970) pp. 19–32. This article, and another by Thirlwall in the *Yorkshire Bulletin of Economic and Social Research* (1969), has a similar purpose to Archibald's study [27] in that the intention is to evaluate the potential contribution of reductions in regional unemployment differentials to national counter-inflationary policies. However, the approach is more disaggregated and, although the results confirm that a more even distribution of unemployment would reduce inflation, Thirlwall concludes that the abandonment of national wage bargaining would have a more substantial effect.

In addition to these articles, there are useful discussions of the strategy of regional economic policy in McCrone [55] and Richardson [23].

PLANNING TECHNIQUES

[36] G. C. Archibald, 'Regional Multiplier Effects in the U.K.', *Oxford Economic Papers* (Mar 1967) pp. 22–45. Knowledge of regional multiplier values helps in assessing the impact on aggregate demand of injections into the regional economy. Archibald relies partly on 'armchair empiri-

cism' in deriving feasible ranges for minimum values for U.K. regions. The problem with the aggregate multiplier concept is that it cannot take account of the fact that multiplier effects vary according to the sector where the injection occurs.

[37] B. R. Berman, B. Chinitz and E. M. Hoover, *Projection of a Metropolis*, Technical Supplement to the New York Metropolitan Region Study (Harvard U.P., Cambridge, Mass., 1961). A good example of the use of population and employment forecasting techniques. Forecasts are made of both the aggregate growth and its intra-regional distribution.

[38] J. R. Boudeville, *Problems of Regional Economic Planning* (Edinburgh U.P., 1966). Many different planning techniques are considered, with particular emphasis on the importance of regional delineation. The last two chapters describe regional planning in France.

[39] J. B. Cullingworth and S. C. Orr, *Regional and Urban Studies* (Allen & Unwin, London, 1969). A useful collection of articles on regional planning. Topics covered include labour market planning, population and employment projection, housing markets and urban transport planning.

[40] F. B. Gillie, *Basic Thinking in Regional Planning* (Mouton, The Hague, 1967). This is a non-technical planners' guide, including much common sense but little economic analysis.

[41] C. D. Harris, 'Methods of Research in Economic Regionalisation', *Geographia Polonica*, no. 4: *Methods of Economic Regionalisation* (Warsaw, 1964) pp. 59–86. A general survey of techniques of defining regions. Other articles in the same volume provide interesting case studies.

[42] W. Isard, *Methods of Regional Analysis* (M.I.T. Press, Cambridge, Mass., 1960). This is the standard text on techniques. Chapters include population and migration projection, social accounts and balance of payments at the regional level, multiplier analysis, input–output analysis, industrial complex analysis and inter-regional linear programming.

[43] W. Isard, E. W. Schooler and T. Vietorisz, *Industrial Complex Analysis and Regional Development* (M.I.T. Press,

Cambridge, Mass., 1959). Industrial complex analysis focuses attention on the interrelationships between industries and the varying need for locational proximity. Most of the book concerns the selection of linked industrial groups suitable for establishment in Puerto Rico.

[44] E. Nevin, A. R. Roe and J. I. Round, *The Structure of the Welsh Economy*, Welsh Economic Studies, no. 4 (Cardiff, 1966). An interesting example of constructing an input–output table with incomplete data.

[45] D. B. Steele, 'Regional Multipliers in Great Britain', *Oxford Economic Papers* (July 1969) pp. 268–92. This is an attempt to estimate multipliers for U.K. regions from various data on inter-regional freight flows, and some interesting differences are revealed, confirming in general the earlier estimates of Archibald [36]. The main criticism must relate to the assumption that value/weight ratios are identical for all regions.

[46] A. P. Thirlwall, 'A Measure of the Proper Distribution of Industry', *Oxford Economic Papers* (Mar 1967) pp. 46–58. Thirlwall describes the technique of shift and share analysis: see also Perloff, Dunn, Lampard and Muth [63]. In applying this to U.K. regions he finds that there is relatively little evidence to suggest that regional policy has been successful in securing 'a proper distribution of industry'.

REGIONAL POLICY IN INDIVIDUAL COUNTRIES

There are numerous studies of the United Kingdom and its constituent regions, reflecting not so much the intensity of the problem as the relatively long history of intervention and the variety of policy instruments tried. The reviews of the joint-stock banks have featured many articles on regional policy, and some of these have already been referred to. The following have been drawn from other sources and together provide many valuable insights.

[47] A. J. Brown, 'Surveys of Applied Economics: Regional Economics, with Special Reference to the United Kingdom', *Economic Journal* (Dec 1969) pp. 759–95. Brown's

article summarises valuable research undertaken at the National Institute of Economic and Social Research as well as other studies of the U.K. regional problem.

[48] J. R. Cable, 'Regional Policy and the Location of Industry', in *The U.K. Economy: A Manual of Applied Economics*, ed. A. R. Prest (Weidenfeld & Nicolson, London, 1966) pp. 166–71. This is a very brief summary of policy in the U.K. and possible criticisms, but it is useful because it considers the implications of non-maximising locational choices for the choice of policy instruments.

[49] G. C. Cameron and B. D. Clark, *Industrial Movement and the Regional Problem*, University of Glasgow Social and Economic Studies, Occasional Paper No. 5 (Oliver & Boyd, Edinburgh, 1966). A report on a major survey of mobile firms. The main emphasis is on the causes of movement and the nature of the location choice, rather than the success (or otherwise) of moves.

[50] Confederation of British Industry, *C.B.I. Regional Study: Regional Development and Distribution of Industry Policy* (Sep 1968). The general approach is predictably biased towards removing the shackles from industrial development. Also, as noted in the text, the argument is not wholly consistent. Nevertheless it provides an interesting critique of the present policies.

[51] Labour Party, *Report of the Study Group on Regional Planning Policy* (Transport House, London, 1970). This is the most thoughtful of the publications by the political parties. The main proposal is of a zone system of the kind discussed by Brown in his note of dissent to the Hunt Report [57], with incentives and disincentives mainly in the form of payroll taxes and subsidies. Increased use of the public sector in regional policy is also proposed, including extensions of public ownership which might well appear less attractive on the other side of the House!

[52] D. Law, 'Industrial Movement and Locational Advantage', *Manchester School* (May 1964) pp. 131–54. This report on a small sample of firms establishing factories in Northern Ireland complements the larger studies of Loasby [53] and Luttrell [54]. In particular it confirms the negative approach to moving (mainly in response

to labour shortages or difficulty with premises), although results (in terms of relative profitability) appeared satisfactory.

[53] B. J. Loasby, 'Making Location Policy Work', *Lloyds Bank Review* (Jan 1967) pp. 34–47. Loasby's survey of about 200 firms moving out of Birmingham to Development Areas and overspill reception areas reveals many characteristics of location choice. In particular, it emphasises that moves usually occur in response to crisis situations, that search procedures are extremely limited and that more attention is paid to initial rather than long-run costs at alternative sites.

[54] W. F. Luttrell, *Factory Location and Industrial Movement* (N.I.E.S.R., London, 1962). This is the report on a major investigation of the cause, process and consequences of locational choice of selected U.K. firms. Vol. 1 is a general discussion of the results of the inquiry, while vol. 2 contains full details of the industry case studies.

[55] G. McCrone, *Regional Policy in Britain*, University of Glasgow Social and Economic Studies (Allen & Unwin, London, 1969). The outstanding book on British regional policy. McCrone describes the development of policy and discusses the merits and demerits of the various instruments used. Special attention is also paid to the case for a growth-area policy, the problems of regional planning, and of possible entry into the EEC. There is also a chapter on regional economic theory which is useful, albeit largely unrelated to the rest of the text.

[56] R. J. Nicholson, 'The Regional Location of Industry', *Economic Journal*, LXVI (1956) 467–81. This article is now very much out of date, but does constitute a serious attempt to assess the loss of efficiency caused by regional policies which interfere with the free location of industry. However, his argument that those industries with low localisation coefficients are most suitable for relocation is suspect: spatially dispersed industries may be those serving a purely local market whose product, either because of high transport/unit cost or by their very nature (e.g. services), is not transportable. The industries most suited to movement associated with policies of regional diversification will be those serving larger market areas,

and these may currently be the most localised for a variety of economic/historical reasons.

[57] *Report of the Committee on the Intermediate Areas* (the Hunt Report), Cmnd 3998 (H.M.S.O., London, 1969). The most recent overall review of the U.K. regional problem and in particular of the difficulties faced by the 'grey areas'. Not for the first time in U.K. committee reports, the best part is to be found in the notes of dissent at the back. It is here that Brown argues the case, *inter alia*, for a broader approach to regional policy including the introduction of congestion taxes in areas where there is physical congestion as well as pressure on the labour market.

There is a considerable volume of published material on regional policy in other countries. References to some case studies are given in Friedmann and Alonso [10] pp. 716–18. Further studies of area development, with a bias towards demonstrating the application of formal models, are to be found in the *Papers and Proceedings of the Regional Science Association* and the *Journal of Regional Science*.

A small but balanced selection from the literature is given below.

[58] K. Allen and M. C. Maclennan, *Regional Problems and Policies in Italy and France*, University of Glasgow Social and Economic Studies (Allen & Unwin, London, 1970). Regional problems in Italy and France are more strongly centred on problems of underdevelopment than in the U.K., and this is particularly problematic in Italy because of the relatively high population densities in the backward regions. The development of policies is clearly explained, with frequent comparisons with British experience.

[59] T. N. Brewis, *Regional Economic Policies in Canada* (Macmillan, Toronto, 1969). Canada faces a regional problem which in terms of income and unemployment differentials is greater than that of most European nations. Brewis describes, *inter alia*, the particular problems faced by the Atlantic Provinces, and the various measures introduced to secure more balanced regional development. Success has been limited, and the association between unequal

opportunities and ethnic groups introduces a further regrettable dimension of the regional problem.

[60] J. Friedmann, *Regional Development Policy: A Case Study of Venezuela* (M.I.T. Press, Cambridge, Mass., 1966). The first part of this book is concerned with the process of regional development. Friedmann's thesis is that the spatial organisation of the economy changes with the stage of national development and that policy towards developing nations requires recognition of the centre–periphery distinction introduced by Myrdal [19]. The second section applies these conceptual issues to the Venezuelan economy, emphasising the need to channel investment into 'core' regions in an attempt to counteract the tendencies towards regional imbalance.

[61] F. Meyers (ed.), *Area Redevelopment Policies in Britain and the Countries of the Common Market* (U.S. Department of Commerce and Area Redevelopment Administration, U.S. Government Printing Office, Washington, 1965). This is a useful collection of essays on policies in individual countries, albeit now somewhat outdated. The essay by Klaassen on the Benelux countries, cited earlier in relation to the discussion on congestion problems, is included here.

[62] Organisation for European Co-operation and Development, *The Regional Factor in Economic Development* (OECD, Paris, 1970). This is the most recent appraisal of regional policy measures in Western Europe. As a progress report, it is encouraging, but there are important reservations concerning, *inter alia*, the patchiness of results, the continuing problems of congestion associated with big-city magnetism, and the importance of the tertiary sector.

[63] H. S. Perloff, E. S. Dunn, Jr, E. E. Lampard and R. F. Muth, *Regions, Resources and Economic Growth*, published for Resources for the Future Inc. (Johns Hopkins Press, Baltimore, 1960). This is a major study of economic development in the United States since 1870, seeking to explain the forces underlying trends in average regional incomes. Recurrent use is made of the standardisation procedure known as shift and share analysis which is used to separate proportionality shifts (reflecting regional structure) from differential effects (a residual category).

[64] J. G. Williamson, 'Regional Inequality and the Process of National Development: A Description of the Patterns', *Economic Development and Cultural Change*, xiii (1965) 3–45. This is an excellent empirical study of regional inequalities in per capita incomes in various countries. Both cross-sectional and time-series approaches are used and both methods confirm the tendencies for regional inequalities first to increase and later to decrease with the process of national development. The main problem is that the effect on regional inequalities of government intervention is not isolated.